AI AND THE OCTOPUS ORGANIZATION

An urgent call to rethink company leadership, culture, and growth strategy. This is essential reading for the world's AI business transformation journey.

—Anish Shah
CEO of Mahindra Group and Past President,
Indian Federation of Chambers of Commerce & Industry

AI and the Octopus Organization is a timely and insightful guide for leaders navigating enterprise transformation. It offers a compelling vision for building agile, resilient organizations—and turns that vision into action through practical frameworks and vivid examples. Brill and Wunker bring clarity to a complex topic and help leaders think bigger about what's possible in an AI-enabled world.

—Mojgan Lefebvre
Chief Information and Operations Officer, Travelers

Wow! Practical, powerful, and fun to read. I highly recommend *AI and the Octopus Organization*.

—Scott D. Anthony
Clinical Professor, Tuck School of Business, Dartmouth

AI and the Octopus Organization cuts through AI hype to deliver actionable frameworks for organizational change. Using the octopus as a model for distributed intelligence, the book presents concrete strategies for decentralized decision-making, real-time information flow, and adaptive leadership. The book's strength lies in its practical approach—real case studies, clear methodologies, and specific implementation guidance rather than abstract ideas. The biological metaphor works well because it focuses on survival and adaptation, not just efficiency gains. For executives facing AI disruption, this provides a roadmap for restructuring organizations to remain competitive. For organizations that already leverage AI, it provides a source of insights to accelerate the path to value creation.

—Euro Beinat
Global Head of AI, Prosus Group and Naspers

In my work with AI initiatives worldwide, the hardest part has never been the technology—it's knowing how and where to apply it. This book gets that exactly right.

—Johan Harvard
Global AI Advisory Lead, Tony Blair Institute for Global Change

Published by Menlo Park Books

Cover design by William Hoffman and Cary Janks

Interior design by THINK Book Works

AI

and the
OCTOPUS ORGANIZATION

**Building the
Superintelligent Firm**

Jonathan Brill
&
Stephen Wunker

MENLO
PARK

CONTENTS

Foreword   v

Introduction: Why Transform?   vii
Bang. Everything Changed.

The Current and Future State of AI

CHAPTER 1   **Reimagining Growth Amid a Sea Change**   3
Small innovations lead to big transformation

Anatomy of the Octopus Organization

CHAPTER 2   **Eight Arms**   23
Lift front-line teams and reinvent management by distributing decisions

CHAPTER 3   **Neural Necklace**   41
Unite knowledge, coordinate innovation, and boost agility

CHAPTER 4   **Three Hearts**   53
Adapt to shifting needs with the right leadership toolkit

CHAPTER 5   **RNA-Powered Resilience**   67
Accelerate action and frontline innovation through accurate sensing

Setting the Right Culture

CHAPTER 6 **An Emotional Being** 81
Embrace disruption by building trust

CHAPTER 7 **Strategic Serendipity** 91
Increase success by leaning into uncertainty

Beginning Your Journey

CHAPTER 8 **Your Transformation Plan** 105
*Lead your AI transformation with a
step-by-step roadmap*

Appendix 119
Scaling Enterprise AI

About the Authors 125

Acknowledgments 127

References 131

Index 137

FOREWORD

By seamlessly blending history, biology, and technology, the authors guide us through a journey from the extinction of the dinosaurs to the future of work transformed by AI. Inspired by the resilience and agility of the octopus, they paint a picture of a superintelligent organization in which humans and AI collaborate seamlessly to create sustainable hyper performance.

As you might expect from the world's leading futurist and the developer of one of the world's first smartphones, this is not a dry "how to" textbook on AI and change management; it's a colorful intellectual canvas that forces us to rethink everything we thought we knew about organizational agility and the art of the possible. To achieve this, the authors utilize a surprisingly wide pallet of ideas and facts, seamlessly blending their perspectives on everything from serendipity to strategy with tangible and actionable transformational advice, sprinkling all of it with vivid, real-life examples. Just like the octopus that inspired them, this is a book with both brain and (multiple) hearts that will survive the test of time.

—Pär Edin
Former Board Committee Chair, KPMG LLP and KPMG AI Leader

INTRODUCTION: WHY TRANSFORM?

Bang. Everything Changed.

ixty-six million years ago, an asteroid the size of Manhattan struck the Yucatán Peninsula with the energy of ten billion Hiroshima bombs. Massive clouds of toxic dust blotted out the sun, cooled the planet, and generated torrents of acid rain. Within weeks, 75 percent of Earth's species were on the road to extinction.

Before the asteroid, the prehistoric oceans had been diverse, life-rich biomes, teeming with thousands of species of a creature seldom considered today: the ammonite. Today we have only their fossilized shells, intricately coiled and ranging in size from a few inches to several feet in diameter. The ammonite's evolution had been so gradual and consistent that geologists use their fossils to date rock strata.

The ammonite's success was built on an unyielding design. Its protective shell, formed by slow changes over millions of years, was perfectly adapted for a predictable, stable environment. But in a brutal twist of fate, the very rigidity that had once ensured the ammonite's dominance would lead to its extinction. The acid rain that washed over the oceans following the meteor strike dissolved the delicate shells of its young and devastated its primary food source, plankton.

But amid the ruin, a story of survival emerged—one that would come to define resilience in the face of radical disruption: the octopus. Unlike the ammonite, the octopus's physiology enables it to transform far faster than it can evolve. Its soft, malleable body is capable of extraordinary feats. It changes color in an instant, squeezes through seemingly impassable gaps, and even regenerates lost limbs. A secret advantage lies in its ability to reconfigure its RNA, a mechanism that allows it to adjust its genetic code in hours. While the ammonite's evolution was measured by a gradual march, the octopus is a master of rapid, continuous transformation. When its environment was thrown into chaos, it changed its biological processes to thrive.

This ancient drama of extinction and survival offers a powerful metaphor for today's business landscape. Like ammonites, many companies have evolved rigid and hierarchical structures optimized for incremental, predictable change. These organizations thrived in eras when steady growth and minor adjustments were sufficient. But in a world subject to disruptions that arrive with the force of an asteroid, those rigid, time-tested models are fatal.

Today, artificial intelligence is emerging as the catalyst for a fundamental shift that will redefine whole industries and economies. ChatGPT, Grok, Gemini, and DeepSeek are merely the opening acts.

AI's evolution is not linear but exponential, a seismic event measured on a Richter scale. Small percentage improvements in AI performance are rapidly compounding into transformative shifts. Over the coming five years, the current best AI models could cost one hundred-thousandth of what they do today, based on linear projections. By 2030, we could see a thirtyfold increase in output quality. In practical terms, these enhancements mean that tasks once deemed too intractable or too expensive to automate can now be accomplished with unprecedented speed and efficiency. The impossible and the unaffordable are becoming feasible and cheap at eye-popping rates. In just a few short months, AI's competitive coding performance has risen from the sixtieth percentile compared with elite human programmers to near perfection.[1]

Much more is coming. Even now, AI has agentic capabilities, meaning it can take action without human intervention. In a number of cities, self-driving cars roam the streets. That is one of the first major examples of a service becoming software. Soon, you will be able to buy most every knowledge service as software. Tell your AI what you want accomplished and when, and it can work with other agents (and people) to manage the rest. The step from executing relatively simple personal tasks to performing more complex business operations is in technological terms—not all that vast. When AI bridges from remarkable thinking to remarkable semiautonomous action, the possibilities explode.

The AI debate often fixates on *artificial superintelligence*—the day machines outthink every human. That milestone, impressive as it sounds, isn't the real turning point. We humans dominate the planet not because we hold the most collective neurons (an ant colony wins that contest) but because we coordinate our actions across distance and centuries. Language, culture, and organization weave individual talents into shared achievement, empowering us to build cities, redirect rivers, and raise living standards generation after generation.

AI's breakthrough lies in *amplifying* that human coordination, not replacing it. Algorithms already excel at many isolated tasks. AI's decisive edge is the ability to knit our scattered insights, plans, and decisions into fluid, real-time collaboration. Picture a voluntary, always-on network that extends each person's expertise, letting diverse teams spark ideas and act faster than any hierarchy alone can.

Crucially, we don't need sci-fi breakthroughs to unlock this potential. The tools exist today. What lags is organizational imagination: redesigning roles, incentives, and safeguards so people and machines can think together at scale while preserving autonomy and creativity. When we do, AI becomes less a central brain issuing orders and more a catalyst that lets individuals achieve together what no one could even attempt alone.

That opportunity, and how to seize it, is the focus of this book.

The change that AI is driving will not follow a linear progression; it is scaling in multiple directions and all at once. The lesson is clear: rigid, unyielding business structures are destined for extinction. Just like the ammonite, organizations that cling to outdated structures will perish. If organizations want to survive, they must become fluid like the octopus.

Here's the happy irony that underlies this book: While AI is forcing this transformation, it also makes it possible.

WHAT THIS BOOK IS ABOUT

Over the next five years, the gap between companies that integrate AI and those that merely experiment with it will spell the difference between survival and extinction. This book is your blueprint for changing the nature of your management and organization to best adapt to an AI-infused world.

To be clear, we are not talking about chatbots, although they're a small piece of the puzzle. When we write about AI, we mean technology that supports decisions, manages communication, simulates options, and enables vast amounts of data to be filtered to the right people at the most opportune moments. This technology is already a reality, even if its deployment is uneven among organizations today.

As a leader, you can't assume that your organization will somehow be immune to the coming disruptions of AI. Nor should you hope that AI will influence all companies in the same ways and you will have the luxury of picking from a smorgasbord of best practices. In fact, it's the divergence among firms that creates the opportunity.

AI is a juggernaut, and it is accelerating at an exponential pace. Now is the time to ask and answer the question, "What will our enterprise look like in five years?" Because the changes you will need to make require time, and if you wait five years to start, it will be too late.

It might be tempting to adopt a conservative, wait-and-see approach, using AI-powered automation to hone your decision-making and eliminate some overhead while learning from other companies' mistakes. This approach ignores the challenges AI poses to inflexible, top-down organizations, as well as the new and better ways of managing that it already enables. AI will allow some organizations to grow to massive size and others to shrink to more manageable proportions as they become profitable nodes in a broad ecosystem of partners. "AI-ifying" the status quo is a path to extinction. We have to be bolder to leverage what's possible.

For all the very real uncertainties about how AI will evolve and the risks it may pose, we believe that there is a right path to take. Use AI to:

- ▸ Distribute and speed routine decision-making
- ▸ De-silo your functions and management
- ▸ Develop a keener sense of both your competitive environment and your own enterprise

That's how you become an Octopus Organization™. Your organization will not just be more resilient and able to adapt to external changes—it will be smarter and more able to experiment, learn, and take calculated risks.

WHY WE WROTE THIS BOOK

As innovation practitioners, we've spent our careers guiding our own and our clients' teams through periods of disruptive change, helping them become disruptors themselves, developing new products and frontline technologies, identifying major opportunities, and growing rapidly into new markets.

Jonathan Brill is the Futurist-in-Residence at Amazon, Executive Chairman of the Center for Radical Change, and former Global Futurist and Research Director at HP. *Forbes* calls him "the world's leading futurist." As an AI Lab Chief, technology executive, and creative director at Frog Design, his teams have developed over 350 products, generating tens of billions of dollars in new revenue for clients. As a consultant and board advisor, he has guided multinational corporations and national governments, as well as frontier tech firms working in AI, defense, food, and advanced manufacturing.

Stephen Wunker is the Managing Director of New Markets Advisors, a global consulting firm that develops growth strategies for ambitious innovators, including 29 of the Fortune 500. A pioneer in mobile marketing and payments, he led the development of one of the world's first smartphones. As a longtime collaborator with the late Clayton Christensen, Harvard Business School's legendary scholar of business disruption, Stephen played a key role in refining and applying his theories of Disruptive Innovation and Jobs to be Done. He has worked across sectors to help large organizations identify major opportunities and move quickly, despite legacy systems or cultural resistance.

During the many times we've helped our clients navigate their AI transformation efforts, we've noticed two key problems. First, there is little consensus on how to structure and manage organizations in the AI Age. Some argue that AI will incentivize a core leadership team to consolidate decision-making, while others predict it will incentivize radical democratization. Some studies show that AI entrenches whatever leadership style is already in place, whether centralized or decentralized.[2] Second, even several years after ChatGPT made its debut in 2022, clients are struggling to turn localized AI pilots into broader organizational transformations. As a result, teams often run surface-level experiments that lead nowhere. Organizations need to embrace AI's disruptions, not retrofit them in a futile attempt to maintain what's familiar.

AI and the Octopus Organization presents an actionable vision of the kind of organization that is best prepared to succeed in the AI Age, and offers practical tools that can make that vision a reality. The book is based on our work as pioneers and doers as well as on in-depth discussions with more than fifty leaders in AI, academia, and industry. We studied dozens of organizations that are moving concertedly in the direction of AI, assessed over two million workforce surveys conducted with the Harrison Assessment team, and did the tough spadework to discover what worked and what did not, to distill fact from hype.

Most books on AI-led management feel like technical manuals. This one is different: We turn breakthrough research into plain language, animate it with real-world cases, and show you companies that are already rewiring themselves for an AI-enabled future, so your organization can move just as decisively. We do not presume you are the CEO—wherever you sit in an organization, you'll find content that's relevant.

YOUR TRANSFORMATION GUIDE

The AI Transformation Overview

CHAPTER	CORE POINT	WHAT YOU WILL LEARN	SAMPLE STRATEGIC ACTION
1. Reimagining Growth	AI recombines labor, capital, and energy costs; growth curves bend upward for early movers.	The key macro issues that make AI-enabled organizational change a necessity, not a luxury.	Reconsider your strategy and what you must excel at doing.
2. Eight Arms	Push everyday decisions to AI-equipped frontline teams, freeing leadership to steer big bets.	How to delegate decision-making and judgment while maintaining alignment and brand consistency.	Grant edge teams data, micro-budgets, and clear risk bands so approvals vanish from routines.
3. Neural Necklace	Create seamless horizontal communication across teams.	How to work with AI to decentralize and make context-rich information universally discoverable in real time.	Invest in a searchable data repository that pushes tailored insights to every role.
4. Three Hearts	Master three operating modes—analytic, agile, aligned—and switch deliberately as conditions change.	Modes of leadership that avoid both command-and-control relapse and free-for-all agile anarchy.	Codify triggers that pause analysis, launch bursts, or reconvene teams for cultural recalibration.
5. RNA-Powered Resilience	Empower rapid-rewrite squads that sense shocks early and update processes in real time.	How to turn resilience into a standing capability instead of an expensive post-crisis recovery project.	Authorize cross-functional crews to tweak pricing, workflow, or channels within hours—not quarters.

(continued)

CHAPTER	CORE POINT	WHAT YOU WILL LEARN	SAMPLE STRATEGIC ACTION
6. An Emotional Being	Culture shifts when you rewrite roles, change incentives, and redeploy talent.	How to overcome the trust issues that silently kill AI transformations.	Revise job designs and rewards first; then frame AI as a career mobility accelerator.
7. Strategic Serendipity	Leverage ways of working that let AI stack the odds in your favor.	Ways to convert uncertainty from threat into a managed asset by making optionality a measurable KPI.	Add KPIs that track idea flow, diverse collaborations, and fast, risk-balanced experiments.
8. Your Transformation Plan	The detailed path to move from vision to organizational transformation.	The step-by-step approach to managing AI transformation.	Require every experiment to earn a "right to scale" and model daily AI use in leadership.

This book is broken into four parts.

The Current and Future State of AI. Chapter 1, "Reimagining Growth Amid a Sea Change," outlines the current state of AI and looks to the future, unpacking how AI will transform societies and markets. It sets the frame from which the Octopus Organization emerges.

Anatomy of the Octopus Organization. Chapters 2 through 5 present the four pillars of the Octopus Organization based on biological traits of the octopus. Chapter 2, "Eight Arms," outlines a model for distributive decision-making that empowers frontline staff to take greater initiative and act more strategically, revolutionizing the role of middle management. Chapter 3, "Neural Necklace," describes new means of communication that keep all parts of the organization aligned. Chapter 4, "Three Hearts," describes a multitracked leadership style that adjusts to rapid changes in priorities, challenges, and market forces. Finally, Chapter 5, "RNA-Powered Resilience" describes how your organization can more effectively and rapidly sense external threats, while democratizing experimentation to continue to push the envelope.

Setting the Right Culture. Simply changing the structure of your organization is not enough. Success depends on the trust you build with your workforce. Earning this trust requires a cultural shift, an organization-wide willingness to embrace the unknown and leave familiar ways of working behind. In Chapter 6, "An Emotional Being," we offer practical strategies—built on what we've learned from millions of career development surveys—for fostering a culture that embraces change. Chapter 7, "Strategic Serendipity," highlights a seemingly counterintuitive benefit of Octopus Organizations: habits and tools that increase "luck" and stack the odds in favor of success.

Beginning Your Journey. Finally, and critically, in Chapter 8, "Your Transformation Plan," we provide you with the concrete steps to take to develop your transformation plan and get it underway. If you read just one chapter, make sure it's this one.

The tide has turned. The organizations that own the future will be the ones that throw off their shells and swim with the octopuses. We will begin in Chapter 1 by charting AI's trajectory over the coming five years, the window you have to rearchitect your company before the true sea change arrives.

Ready? Let's dive in.

THE CURRENT AND FUTURE STATE OF AI

Reimagining Growth Amid a Sea Change

Small innovations lead to big transformation

"AI will be the most transformative technology of the 21st century. It will affect every industry and aspect of our lives."

—JENSEN HUANG

Newton, Kansas, 1884. A telegraph clicks its way across the prairies: "NO 1 ENG 23 MEET SECOND 2 ENG 30 AT NEWTON." The train crew at Newton springs into action, halting a carriage of timber heading for Chicago as the 7:15 p.m. express to Los Angeles barrels along its evening journey. Seconds later, the timber carriage is back on its way eastward. This story repeats itself hundreds of times an hour all across the United States: a network of dispatchers and stationmasters coordinating hundreds of miles of movement using only Morse code and synchronized watches.

To run at the speed of the telegraph, railway companies didn't just build tracks. They built a management system. That system assumed three things:

- ▸ **No real-time feedback.** Most workers had no two-way communication. Their only guide was a timetable and a pocket watch.
- ▸ **No room for judgment.** Workers were not skilled in decision-making. They followed rigid rules because they lacked context.
- ▸ **No visibility into impact.** Decisions made in the field weren't coordinated or simulated for systemic effects. They were isolated actions within a linear chain.

Railroads were managed from the top down. Dispatchers planned and crews executed. Rules, not reflexes, ran the show. That "hub and spoke" model scaled. It became the default structure of the industrial firm, and it's still how most organizations operate today. But the core assumptions that underpin this model are collapsing.

Jump to Topeka, just down the line from Newton, in 2030. A startup, T-Town Treats, has transformed an abandoned warehouse into a test bed for innovative frozen foods. The research team relies on AI assistants to scan organizational chatter, surface real-time data, and simulate second-order consequences to develop new product prototypes. The marketing team leans on AI agents to anticipate trends, suggest new flavors, redesign packaging, and finalize ad copy. Operations uses AI to manage the supply chain. Everyone can sense, coordinate, and act at speed. Soon, the startup becomes a linchpin of the local dairy industry.

Jane Jensen works at T-Town Treats. She wears glasses all day, but not to correct her vision. Rather, these glasses are her gateway to having AI everywhere. When she has questions, she asks them out loud, and microphones embedded in the glasses relay her query to the cloud. In milliseconds, AI sifts through not only the company's market data and internal correspondence, but also volumes of management best practices culled from the broader world. Tiny speakers near the ears summarize the findings for her, and a head-up display inside the glasses projects key details on the lenses. Her AI agent personified within the system, "Bill," knows the kind of information that's most important to Jane and her changing contexts. He connects her to the right people and software inside the organization at the right time to enable fast, flexible decisions.

The railroad invented the modern firm, and AI is about to reinvent it. Just as the telegraph enabled new structures of time, trust, and control, AI will reshape how we assign agency, coordinate across boundaries, and learn from weak signals. It will remake the norms of organizational management.

This isn't sci-fi. The core technologies are already here, and so is the pressure to use them. The challenge is not technological; it is sociological. How quickly can human organizations adapt? We must redefine what is possible, because keeping pace is no longer enough. Demographic shifts, rising capital costs, and energy constraints—among other disruptions—are reshaping the economic landscape. We need powerful tools to drive efficiency and strategic fluidity.

AI is at once a disruptor and a tool for navigating disruption. To use it well, you must reimagine the way you manage your business.

THE OLD ENGINES OF GROWTH ARE UNDER PRESSURE

We recognize that organizational transformation is hard, and it should be avoided if the status quo can hold. But we live in a time of accelerating change. To thrive, organizations must increase their speed and adaptability. Simply treading water will eventually cause them to drown.

The great disruptor isn't AI alone. It's a combination of at least four separate trends stacked with it: shrinking talent pools, costlier capital, fragile energy supplies, and jittery geopolitics. Like a rogue wave that forms when winds, tides, and ocean currents collide and interact, their combined force can flip any company that was built for calm water.[3] Leaders who spot the crest early and ride it will shoot forward while other boats are swamped.

No company can surf every rogue wave, but you can read the currents and avoid getting broadsided, and that skill is your edge. Let's take a closer look at each of those four trends.

Labor Scarcity

By 2030, the working-age population in the industrialized nations of the G7 is projected to shrink by 5 percent. As birthrates fall and retired populations grow, the pool of available talent will decrease. Organizations are forced to ask: How can we do more with fewer hands? The answer is *by leveraging AI to automate routine tasks and free up skilled workers for higher-value roles.* Leaders can prepare now by addressing capability gaps before they affect execution. Siemens, for example, is using large language models to codify expertise from veteran machinists into standard operating procedures, reducing new-hire onboarding time from eighteen months to eight as vital knowledge becomes more accessible when it is needed. This expands the talent pool Siemens can consider for a particular role and reduces the costs of training.

It has become trendy to say that AI will exclusively augment what employees can currently do with minimal impacts on demand for labor, but this is a crowd-pleasing fiction. Let's accept the reality: AI fundamentally changes where labor is best deployed. It doesn't need to end employment by any means, but it will alter the nature of work for most roles in many industries. This means you need to think differently about what skills will be needed in the workplace of the future and how AI can help bridge those gaps.

Capital Constraints

From 2020 to 2024, the ten-year US Treasury yield fluctuated between 0.52 percent (August 2020) and over 5.0 percent (October 2023), levels not seen since the early 2000s. Each 50-basis-point rate surprise can reduce the net present value of a five-year investment project by approximately 2.5 percent. With this kind of financial uncertainty, companies must rethink how they deploy funds, potentially reducing long-term bets that tie up investments and finding ways to make operational spending more fluid. AI can help by streamlining processes, enhancing efficiency, and enabling tight external partnerships.

Energy and Infrastructure

Behind every AI breakthrough is a vast network of data centers and computational resources. These systems are hungry, demanding vast amounts of energy that strain power grids. By 2030, data centers may account for 20 percent of total global energy demand.[4] As data centers become more and more critical to business operations, their locations and efficiencies will become key competitive factors. Given the lengthy time horizons to both establish data centers and expand grid capacity, your organization will be pressured to use its existing computing power in more efficient ways. More broadly, the AI race is putting greater pressure on our energy systems. Access to affordable and reliable sources of energy will become increasingly restricted, absent large-scale investments in grid expansion and electrification.

Geopolitical Dynamics

The economic order that has existed since the end of World War II is shifting. Export controls, talent restrictions, and competitive pressures are fragmenting technology ecosystems. Companies must contend with policies and regulations that influence not only where they source components but how they access critical data and talent. As protectionism continues to increase, organizations must build resilience into their supply chains and factor in geopolitics as they act.

Turbulence doesn't need to be harmful to your business, so long as you adapt. For leaders, the challenge is to transform these constraints into opportunities. More than a temporary fix, AI is the backbone of a new strategy.

AI AS THE NEW PATH TO GROWTH

AI is not just another software upgrade; it offers a radical reimagining of growth. Rather than merely speeding and automating existing tasks, AI rebalances labor, capital, and energy, the traditional inputs of growth. With fewer workers available and capital investments under tighter scrutiny, AI can unlock new sources of productivity, transforming rigid cost centers into fluid, digitally-driven operations that enable businesses to do more with less.

Consider Procter & Gamble's approach at one of its Berlin facilities.[5] By integrating a system of AI-powered sensors into its production lines, quality is monitored continuously instead of in batches. This not only improves the output and reduces waste, it also frees employees to carry out less repetitive, higher-value labor. AI converted a cost center into a profit engine by freeing labor and resources to do more productive work.

AI is already a competitive necessity, and it will become more-so every day. The analogy to the rise of the internet is clear. In the mid-1990s, many companies made tentative gestures to adapt, such as putting sales materials onto (diabolically ugly) websites. By the turn of the millennium, however, they were rushing pell-mell to set up new internet-powered businesses and operating models. They hurried up because competition was forcing their hands. Of course, much money was wasted during that rush, and many new entrants still succeeded in disrupting the slower-moving old guard. It is far healthier to have a multiyear, phased transition to new models, which is why the time to plan your AI transition is right now.

Companies' AI-enabled leaps forward will be bounded by constraints, and they will compete on their ability to overcome them. The most sophisticated AI systems, for instance, require significant compute power. As they scale, they demand increasingly efficient hardware and smarter resource management. Another constraint is more important: the capacity of an organization to change.

So, what can AI do for you and your team in the near future? Don't start with the technology, start with the value. Ask three questions about the way you and your people spend your days:

What won't humans do? In this category, consider low-value, ignored, or impossible-to-scale work. AI can't always perform miracles, but it is often better than nothing. For example, AI-based HR screening systems have flaws and the potential for systematized bias, yet when used responsibly and with human oversight, they can help companies expand the variety and quality of candidates they screen, updating hiring processes that may not have changed in decades. Unilever, for example, uses AI to analyze videos of job applicants' interviews and game-based assessments, reducing hiring times by 75 percent while improving candidate quality.[6]

What shouldn't humans do? This could include rote, error-prone, or privacy-sensitive tasks. AI will become acceptable at a broad number of tasks in the next two to three years, just as it has already become excellent at roles like fielding routine customer service queries online. For example, project and middle managers fritter away hours of their days in alignment meetings. Today, Zoom, Microsoft, and Otter provide digital assistants that can synthesize meeting takeaways, outline agreed-upon next steps, and highlight unresolved questions. Previously, a team member would need to handle these tasks, and—let's be honest—most teams did without them. While digital assistants' outputs are currently far from perfect, they provide at least some value for a fraction of the time and cost.

What can't humans do? Humans cannot do continuous pattern recognition at a superhuman scale. As a practical matter, AI's ability to retain and iteratively process data is limited more by economics than by technology. Give it enough computing power and it will outperform the physical limits of human cognition in unexpected and non-intuitive ways. For example, digital pathology teams use high-powered slide scanners and AI algorithms to both detect potentially cancerous anomalies in tissue samples and track millions of images so they can be available for remote viewing. Highly trained pathologists are still needed to review outputs and make judgments on potential cases, but they now do so from the comfort of their home offices. Digital pathology significantly reduces the talent and infrastructure bottlenecks for healthcare providers, allowing smaller teams to provide better care for more patients.

It's both exciting and scary to consider how artificial super-intelligence will change our society and the way we work. That technology will come at some point, but your organization should prioritize a different benchmark. Ask yourself, in the next two years:

- ▸ Where will AI-enabled systems be obviously faster, better, and cheaper than your existing processes?
- ▸ What can be automated or augmented for 20 percent of the current, labor-intensive cost?
- ▸ What issues can AI handle that you don't have the capacity for?

AI doesn't need to be perfect to be useful. It only needs to be better than what you're doing now. At the same time, it's developing at such a pace that we need to skate to where the puck is going, so that we have time to get there.

HOW LONG DO YOU HAVE?

Skeptics still mutter that AI hasn't lived up to the hype. That's like judging a hurricane by its first raindrops. Under the surface, AI's capabilities double every few months while its deployment costs plunge. Many of the core technologies of the future are in development; they just aren't well integrated yet. The moment those tools tip from "pilot" to "platform," the gap between early movers and laggards will become a chasm.

Developers we've interviewed at legacy manufacturing firms report a 15 to 20 percent boost in coding efficiency. Leaders at giants like Amazon claim improvements of up to 70 percent in processes. Much of this is due to "Vibe Coding," in which users give AI the gist of what they're looking to accomplish and then sit back while AI carries out the research, pulls together the code libraries, and tweaks the APIs and MCPs (application programming interfaces and model context protocols, which enable software to work with other software). With this technique, AI is moving from simply providing information to using the same tools that human scientists, statisticians, and engineers deploy to test and correct their work.

As AI improves its ability to carry on natural language conversations with non-coders, it will become increasingly useful at writing software to help them accomplish tasks. Software skills are less and less a barrier to the widescale adoption of automation.

Beyond coding, AI-powered tools are transforming the way companies capture and deploy knowledge. Innovations and insights that were developed within one function or geography can become visible across whole enterprises via transcription tools and customized reporting.

Databricks' LakehouseIQ platform, for example, uses AI to integrate enterprise data lakes. This allows organizations to query a range of data sources with natural language. Similarly, Microsoft has combined Copilot and Viva Topics to pull data from Outlook, Teams, SharePoint, and OneDrive and provide contextual search results and auto-generated summaries. As these systems proliferate, the urgent question is no longer which you should adopt. It's how you can use them to meet your organization's specific needs.

AI is already moving from a brainstorming tool that answers simple questions to one that handles far more complex challenges. For instance, both Deepinvent and DeepMind's AI co-scientists make hypotheses, research scientific literature and regulations, and then write patent applications. Other soon-to-be-integrated tools will recommend potential approval paths based on the history of specific patent examiners.

There are many questions that require the insights and knowledge of top-tier advisors. While the best-performing humans may continue to be better, AI can make "good enough" specialist expertise available to people who had neither the money nor time to access it in the past.

Consider the field of process simulation. Organizations working in competitive markets characterized by high stakes and uncertainty often use complex multivariate analysis and game theory to map scenarios. Quantitative hedge funds can stress-test potential positions; an energy supermajor can map the knock-on effects of acquiring a smaller rival. Historically, these types of analyses were unaffordable for all but the largest organizations. Today, high schoolers can do them.

AI is also reinventing project planning. It can absorb the inputs of hundreds or thousands of users, consider external factors and best practices, and weigh second and third order implications to offset risk and optimize for success.

AI is currently limited by the available universe of public data, which has been largely ingested already. But that accounts for only about 1 percent of the data that exists. AI is already moving from a program that simply queries a database, as ChatGPT has historically done. Now, it can search the internet, talk to other AI agents, then coordinate queries into their databases. Accessing other AI models with different data will result in dramatically improved capabilities. Agentic AI then takes things a few steps beyond, taking automated action based on the information found.

By the 2030s, your organization will be able to use AI to run a market analysis for a new consumer electronics product, carry out 80 percent of the electrical and mechanical engineering work, negotiate the price of materials, and work with partners to negotiate deal points for components and processes. Now imagine doing all of that every day instead of every year. How flexible will industries become? How rapidly will change occur?

THE SIX GATES THAT DICTATE YOUR SPEED

Even an octopus can change color only as fast as its skin cells respond to signals. The good news is that, if you understand where technology will slow you down, you can prioritize actions that put you ahead in the right places at the right times. Track these six trends, and you'll know where to press forward and where patience pays.

AI Software Maturity

Big ideas need hardening. Though ChatGPT first shipped in November 2022, its underlying transformer architecture landed on arXiv in June 2017.[7] It typically takes three to five years to move software from research through tool-chain plumbing and safety tuning to enterprise product. Expect a few years of lag between today's grand announcements and collaborative agents that plan, negotiate, and execute inside businesses—much less *between* them.

Look at Allianz's experience with Insurance Copilot. Allianz began a proof-of-concept for a generative AI claims aid in late 2023. Only after a year of audit log, fallback flow, and human-in-the-loop controls did it launch to Austrian motor claims teams.[8]

Edge over Cloud

Insight lives where data is born. Armed with NVIDIA GPUs, Siemens's new industrial computers bring twenty-five-fold faster AI inference to the shop floor. Cameras now flag defects in milliseconds, without any detours to the cloud.[9] While amazing, these products didn't spring up overnight; they were the result of eighteen to twenty-four months of development. Even the most AI-forward manufacturers will need a few more years to retool their plants to use this tech at scale.

Private 5G and Industrial Networks

Swarming agents can't coordinate over sagging Wi-Fi. Siemens and Qualcomm installed the first private standalone 5G network in an industrial setting at the Nuremberg Automotive Test Center back in 2019.[10] Rolling out similar coverage campus-wide still takes about two years per site once spectrum clearances, device certification, and zero-trust overlays are counted. The next generation of space-based and 6G networks won't be available until the 2030s.

Power and Data Center Footprint

Compute is nothing without electrons. Dominion Energy paused new data center hookups in Loudoun County, Virginia, in 2022; a 500 kV transmission upgrade is planned, but it won't clear the queue until 2026.[11] Even "quick fixes" are slow. S&P Global reports lead times for gas turbines of up to seven years, thanks to AI-driven demand.[12] If your roadmap needs virgin megawatts, work with a hyperscaler (a provider of cloud infrastructure like Amazon Web Services) and start the permit dance today. Or architect a strategy that pushes compute to the edge—that is, to the locations where the humans are, where it is harder to regulate power demand.

Human and Institutional Velocity

The slowest code upgrade of all is human culture. It can take years for workforces to incorporate new technologies into their daily routines, and even longer for management practices to make the most of them. We already see patchy uptake of AI at the enterprise level.[13] Disparities in the AI maturity of organizations will only widen as technological progress accelerates. You can close some of the gap by ensuring that AI tools are trusted, that frontline teams integrate them into their daily tasks, and that managers are able to vet the quality of "centaurs" (AI-plus-human outputs).

Organizational Debt

Over time, organizations make decisions, rejig structures, and change processes in ways that solve short-term problems but create long-term bottlenecks, inefficiencies, and cultural liabilities.[14] These build up like a plaque that sticks to every decision or action made within the organization. Latencies created by layers of management can silo the teams that sense change from those that authorize responses. AI makes things worse when rapid change causes teams to favor short-term wins over long-term goals. But it can also help firms reduce organizational debt by revealing inefficiencies, improving decision transparency, breaking down silos, and speeding up approvals.

What AI cannot do (yet) is facilitate the delicate process of devolving decision-making authority and removing layers of management. Those are political decisions, not technical ones. The time it takes to unspool organizational debt depends on how much has built up, but expect a concerted effort to take many months, at the very least.

The technology is here, the timeline on which it can scale is relatively defined, and the interdependencies are well understood—even if capital, energy, infrastructure, and geopolitics will affect them. Whether you choose to lead or fast follow, it's vital that you remove obstacles *before* the next round of opportunities emerges. The future is coming fast, and you will find yourself competing with AI native firms that never had to make this decision.

To begin, ask yourself these questions:

- ▶ Where should you use these technologies to improve processes?
- ▶ Where will you use them to do new things?
- ▶ How will you separate what you have done from what you will do next?

AI Gating Factors

	TIME TO RESOLVE
AI Software Maturity	36–60 months
Edge over Cloud	18–24 months
Private 5G & Industrial Networks	24 months
Data Center and Infrastructure Commissioning	60–120 months
Human & Institutional Velocity	6–36 months
Overcoming Organizational Debt	6–36 months

Three Reasons We Fail to See the Future

The default management best practice is to focus on what you can control and ignore the rest. The problem with this approach is that the world is constantly changing, and when the world changes, what you can control changes too. This is why it really helps to have a picture of how you will compete in a new and different future.

While much about the future is unknowable, you can determine more about it than you might imagine, provided that you have a process. Three key questions can help your organization link today's insights to tomorrow's winning strategy.

1. Are We Using Binoculars Instead of Radar?

It is easy to overfocus on key performance indicators (KPIs), tactics, quarterly performance reports, and analyst objectives. When you concentrate on performance metrics, you're assuming that your goals are still valid. Performance metrics direct us toward conveniently available facts without considering what those facts might mean, when they're looked at in a new context. This is particularly true of officiency-focused organizations that rely heavily on management techniques like Six Sigma.

Does that describe your organization's approach? If so, AI can help you think through larger scenarios and consider second-order effects.

2. Do We Suffer from the Elephant Problem?

Like the proverbial blind men who touch an elephant but are unable to identify what it is, there are times when everyone has some data, but no one has all of the information, or is incentivized to think about the bigger picture. One person feels the elephant's tusk and says it is a spear; another feels its side and thinks it's a wall; a third feels its trunk and declares it is a snake. The phenomenon is particularly true in highly matrixed organizations and multidivisional firms.

If that describes your organization, AI can help by searching for information across your entire enterprise, getting you in touch with the right people, and, in general, providing context about the implications of your decisions.

3. Are We Fighting the Last War?

When organizations ingrain tactics that have worked, they often blind themselves to how changes in context challenge past assumptions. This is particularly true in legacy and highly regulated firms.

Does that describe you? If so, AI can help you overcome your biases so you can see when opportunities have changed—and when your capabilities need to change as well.

How AI Changes Business and Possibility: The Story of Afførd

Throughout the first six chapters of this book, we'll follow the story of a business that integrates AI in ways that lead to radical transformation. The business is fictional, but it is based on a composite of real enterprises. Like IKEA or Ethan Allen, "Afførd" is a vertically integrated furniture manufacturer that operates its own factories, warehouses, and retail stores. As we unpack the Octopus Organization, we'll see how Afførd incorporates its features to change the way work is managed, innovation is fostered, and strategy is built and executed.

For now, consider the ways that AI might change Afførd's strategy and operations. The firm has historically emphasized scale to make its processes as efficient as possible, forcing customers to choose from a small range of offerings within each category. It's vertically integrated, tightly controlling inventory levels throughout production and distribution, and driving demand for exclusive products at its retail locations. This integration allows Afførd to avoid the overhead costs and time that others spend negotiating with external suppliers.

AI changes the company's business logic. In factories, production lines have much greater flexibility and can produce parts in different shapes and sizes. The technology makes it much easier to arrange contracts with outside manufacturers and parts suppliers, reducing overhead costs from external sourcing. It helps with managing inventory levels throughout the supply chain, keeping things efficient no matter who produces the goods. AI-enabled marketing reaches customers via the internet right when they're ready to buy, showing them how products would look in their own homes. This drives demand for priority products and reduces the importance of owning retail stores.

In short, AI challenges Afførd's high-volume, vertically integrated business model. AI allows buyers to customize their furniture, investigate a much broader range of alternatives, and use digital sales and marketing channels to a significantly higher degree. Given the lead time for making investments and building capabilities, if Afførd doesn't acknowledge and act on these fundamental changes quickly, it won't have the opportunity to adjust once the basis of competition has shifted. The disruption will be massive.

ENTER THE OCTOPUS

Your organization is facing a world that is moving faster and less predictably than ever before. AI both contributes to and helps hedge against uncertainty. To fully seize its opportunities, it must be integrated into your organizational structure and management practices in ways that fully leverage its strengths. That's how you transform from an ammonite to an octopus.

In the following chapters, we outline the key features of an Octopus Organization, showing how they function, how you can model them, and who has already adopted them. We start in Chapter 2 with AI's most distinctive and transformative feature: its distributed systems of decision-making.

CHAPTER SUMMARY

AI is not just another IT upgrade. It's a foundational shift. Amid pressures such as labor shortages, increasing capital costs, and geopolitical tension, it enables organizations to reimagine growth. AI's impact will depend on how quickly companies adapt culturally and structurally to integrate it into the core of their operating model.

To stay ahead, leaders must begin their transformation journeys today.

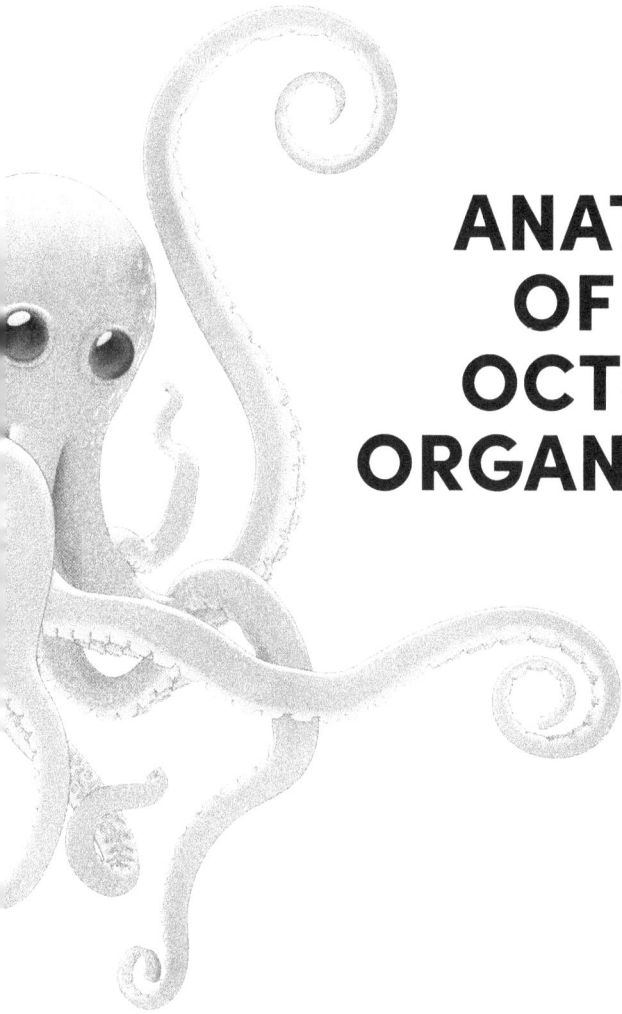

ANATOMY OF THE OCTOPUS ORGANIZATION

CHAPTER 2

Eight Arms

Lift front-line teams and reinvent management by distributing decisions

"If I were thou, I'd call me Us."

—OGDEN NASH
"THE OCTOPUS" (POEM)

Humans sense the world around them, decide whether they need to act, and then move according to signals they receive and process in their brains. The octopus does things differently. It has nine brains—one central brain and a smaller brain for each of its eight arms. An astonishing two-thirds of its neurons are outside of its central brain. Each brain can process inputs and work separately or with the other neural clusters. The nine brains make one mind. In the same way, AI gives all nodes in an organization the ability to monitor what is happening across it, enabling new methods of decision-making and coordination.

THE FOG OF WAR

Until the mid-nineteenth century, Europe's armies consisted of heavily drilled regiments who stood shoulder to shoulder and fought in tightly coordinated formations. Each regiment wore distinctly colored uniforms and carried large banners—not just for show, but to make it easier for senior officers to tell them apart. Surveying the battlefield from a safe distance, those officers gave orders to a retinue of couriers who raced in and out of the action on horseback. Of course, the situation on the ground frequently changed by the time the couriers delivered their commands (if they even managed to get to the front lines), and the regiments were almost impossible to "steer." Once the soldiers started moving in one direction, their fate was set.

Based on his experiences during the Napoleonic Wars, Carl von Clausewitz coined the term "fog of war," a state of extreme uncertainty that impacted every decision and action in battle.[15] Mitigating that uncertainty required meticulous preplanning, inflexible hierarchies, and a culture of unerring order-following, even when it meant marching toward certain death.

By the late nineteenth century, a completely new philosophy of army organization had emerged. Telegraphs and railways created new possibilities for coordinated mobility, collapsing the time that officers previously had to plan and execute strategy. In response, Prussian generals increasingly relied on an organizational philosophy called *Auftragstaktik*, or "mission tactics." Commanders would set objectives and then empower field officers and their units to decide how they should be achieved. This increased real-time adaptability, allowing armies to function more like groups of semi-autonomous cells than large, rigid formations.

The Prussian army effectively restructured its "nervous system" to be more distributed so it could sense and act closer to the action. AI allows your organization to do the same thing.

EMBRACING A NEW NERVOUS SYSTEM

Our technologies define our organizational structures. Bugles, banners, horses, and flags begat rigid hierarchies, low individual autonomy, and plans that were difficult to change once they were set into motion. But organizational structures don't automatically change as new technologies emerge. Even if the will to change them is there, it can be unclear how to best adapt.

The great Prussian general Helmuth von Moltke recognized that telegraphs created new problems even while they solved old ones: More communication doesn't always equal better communication. Telegraphs can spread misinformation more rapidly than word of mouth, for example. This risk convinced von Moltke to further decentralize leadership, because field officers were better placed than staff officers to verify information. But that decision wasn't obvious, and many of von Moltke's colleagues were initially reluctant to devolve their authority.

In the effort to make organizations faster and nimbler, we have flattened them but often failed to evolve them. Too many decisions still get bottlenecked in centralized corporate cortexes. Twenty years ago, business leaders talked a lot about the need to speed the movement from strategy to execution. Then, the idea was to perform strategy and execution simultaneously (agile and continuous delivery). Today, change comes so quickly that execution often occurs before a new strategy is even formulated. The result is an unhealthy rhythm: agile teams sprint ahead, then headquarters slams on the brakes while it attempts to adapt retroactively. Momentum stalls in a spasm of organizational arrhythmia. A new approach is needed.

BUILD YOUR EIGHT ARMS

Organizations with distributed rather than centralized intelligence make many of their decisions from the bottom up rather than the top down. To adjust your organization's nervous system:

- ▸ Use AI to supercharge how people gather data, plan, decide, and act.
- ▸ Devolve power to the qualified staff who are closest to each problem.

Three tactics bring the model to life:

1. **Push cognition to the edge.** Equip every team with real-time data, AI assistance, and the budgetary micro-rights to solve problems instantly. If a customer issue can be fixed in thirty seconds, it should never be queued up for a weekly steering meeting.

2. **Turn the center into a nerve ring, not a command tower.** The C-suite's new job is to set goals, keep standards, and resolve collisions—not micromanage every line item. Like the octopus's central brain, it keeps signals clean and makes conflicts short-lived without throttling its eight limbs' initiatives.

3. **Resynchronize continuously.** Shared metrics, open APIs, and lightweight peer reviews act as the pulse that keeps far-flung experiments in a coherent rhythm. When edge insights reveal a pattern that the core didn't foresee, the whole body pivots to follow.

AI can provide unprecedented contextual awareness, fine-grained decision support, and clear networks of communication at scale. Large language models allow even junior managers to see the wider chessboard that was once the sole province of senior analysts. The systems, when based on appropriate data, bring the right information to the right people at the right time, showing its relevance to the context at hand.

Agents curate data to suit the needs of managers across the firm and ecosystem, digest the information accurately, and spotlight its most critical implications. As managers formulate their responses, AI flags their biases, tests scenarios, and recommends guardrails, all in real time. Software improves executive judgment at every level, allowing even junior staff to make complex and risky decisions with confidence. APIs and agentic frameworks allow the organization's "arms" to trade information laterally, instead of feeding it up or down. Like employees, leaders can also access real-time insight about what is going on across the organization, providing the confidence to remain hands-off.

With AI-supported command, control, and communication, strategy no longer chases execution; both are one.

In Chapter 3 we'll dive deeper into the concept of a neural necklace that coordinates all this activity, but for now remember this principle: *intelligence at the edges, coherence at the core.* Build that, and your company can move like an octopus when the next rogue wave hits.

Not surprisingly, the architects of AI-driven robotic systems have studied octopuses' distributed intelligence. Back in 2017, the Ninth International Conference on Agents and Artificial Intelligence published a paper entitled *The Octopus as a Model for Artificial Intelligence.* "After investigating the behavior of the octopus and the embedded cognition of its arms," its authors wrote, "we can clearly see that the octopus—when viewed as a processing system—is a superb model for efficient cognition."[16] The same principles apply to organizational structures.

Like von Moltke's misgivings about telegraph communications, there will be many reasons that managers of legacy firms will want to slow this shift, not the least of which is the threat it poses to their own power. How much of it must they devolve?

Senior leaders can allay many of their fears by gradual, controlled delegation.

- ▸ In the first stages of the transformation, use AI only on low-risk, high-frequency decisions.
- ▸ Set clear boundaries on what each team can decide alone.
- ▸ Start small and track progress to smooth the shift.
- ▸ Avoid "pilot mode" by linking each early step to broader change.
- ▸ Allow managers to keep a few critical calls; delegate the rest.

CREATING A DISTRIBUTED ORGANIZATION FROM THE BOTTOM UP

Depending on which IT firm's statistics you believe, digital transformations fail to meet their initial objectives 70 to 85 percent of the time. Part of this is because of the executive bauble problem (someone saw something on *Star Trek* and wanted to "make it so"); part of it is because software providers overpromise. Mostly it is because the people who actually had to use the supposedly transformative software weren't involved in the decision-making.

Companies have historically been designed top-down, so software decisions are often made that way. But decentralized decision-making allows for both top-down and bottom-up inputs. The challenge to date has been that the people at the bottom often have neither the communication nor the software skills to participate. Too often, the solution is that an inexperienced consultant breezes in, partially understands the challenge, and hands off requirements to a program manager, who then parses out the job to developers. The poor developers are fated to fail because the problems that need solving have been misstated; also, they likely have no idea what success should look like.

As AI gets better at turning natural speech into code (and it is getting very good at it), folks at the bottom of the management ladder will be able to build prototypes of the software they need and then refine them, even if they don't have computer science degrees. When combined with AI-powered executive judgment and context, their indigenous innovations can be linked into larger programs throughout the enterprise.

Start your AI transformation at the bottom of the ladder. As AI automates repetitive tasks with predictable and discrete outcomes, the responsibilities of your average employee will likely become more human-centered and varied. A bank's risk mitigation team will rely on it for the predictable cases, leaving them to deal with more complex outliers. Imagine a near future where AI brokers automatically negotiate the price and payment terms of suppliers, empowering procurement teams to manage more varied and complicated supply chains. Rather than leading to an "army of drones," AI superpowers your workforce to deal with more variability and ambiguity than ever before.

As junior teams automate rote tasks, make more decisions, and act more strategically, senior managers have two options. They can create complex approval systems so they can maintain oversight and control of the frontline. Or they can empower their workforces to take more initiative by limiting the number of decisions that must be escalated. Of course, we recommend the latter approach.

Look at Stripe, a fintech company that is revolutionizing the way businesses accept payments, manage revenue, and operate globally. In March 2025, Stripe released its Optimized Checkout Suite (OCS), an AI-powered solution that dynamically adjusts payment method ordering and handles fraud intervention.[17] Based on Stripe's extensive payment datasets ($1.4 trillion in annual payment volume), the Optimized Checkout Suite can determine the most relevant payment methods to display based on customer attributes and purchase details, leading to an average 12 percent increase in revenue and a 7 percent increase in conversion rates. The system also dynamically adjusts checkout interventions based on the likelihood of different types of risk. This reduces fraud rates by 30 percent with minimal impacts on conversion.

The system helps customers, but it also removes a category of low-impact, low-skill tasks from Stripe's risk team, allowing them to focus on more nebulous cases. AI increases the volume and complexity of their average workload, but it provides the tools that allow team members to tackle it effectively: a virtuous cycle.

What will a more empowered frontline look like for your organization? It depends on your context, notably your organization's size and risk tolerance. Consider two distinct examples:

▸ Industry giants Siemens and AWS teamed up to build a low-code AI platform that allows production engineers to create software that maximizes factory productivity. They have used it to improve yields, as well as to field suggestions for equipment adjustments and maintenance. Because AI synthesizes complex choices into digestible options, these benefits come with minimal investment in training.[18]

▶ Beyond Better Foods, a food industry innovator founded in 2012, has leveraged AI to pull together insights from voluminous Slack threads, customer conversations, and interactions with suppliers, leading to greater alignment, less time spent chasing information from other teams, and better prioritization of tasks.[19]

In both cases, AI not only augments the skills of frontline staff but also facilitates more streamlined collaboration across the organization.

THE REINVENTION OF THE MIDDLE MANAGER

What is the appropriate role for middle managers if the frontline has greater ownership and decision-making authority? The efficiency gurus may tell you that middle managers will become obsolete and disappear. The opposite is true. AI adoption will reinvent rather than reduce their responsibilities.

Today, middle managers typically spend only a quarter of their time directly supervising and coaching their reports.[20] The rest is spent on administration, advocacy, and alignment. As AI tools proliferate, middle managers will no longer serve as intermediaries between the periphery and the core. Instead, their teams will address a greater share of day-to-day challenges themselves, escalating only the thorniest and most mission-critical issues.

Data from early adopters of AI already bears this out. A recent study by Harvard Business School faculty showed that AI-enabled middle managers involved in computer coding spent 10 percent less of their time on project management and needed to coordinate less with peers. The time savings enabled them to spend 5 percent more time doing actual coding.[21]

Moreover, AI enabled the managers in the study to be better coaches. It provided tools to work more efficiently with low performers on their teams, who ordinarily required inordinate amounts of supervision. This hyperscaled rose garden will still need plenty of tending. Middle managers will need to spend more time upskilling their teams so they can deal with these problems themselves—not to mention managing and improving the AI.

As organizations flatten and functional barriers continue to break down, middle managers will increasingly find themselves:

▸ Leading teams with divergent skill sets
▸ Ensuring that increasingly autonomous teams coordinate effectively
▸ Determining whether AI tools are getting decisions right
▸ Identifying where AI is missing insights that don't show up in the data

In an Octopus Organization, the role of middle managers will include helping their reports to overcome any emotional or educational blocks to AI and learn to use it as effectively as possible. For roles that deal with ambiguity and nondeterministic outcomes (which will be most roles in an Octopus Organization), AI may increase the gulf between the most and least skilled workers.[22] Beware: AI can make junior staff less effective if it sends them down irrelevant "rabbit holes" or feeds them incorrect ("hallucinated") results. Worse, a big risk is using AI's outputs as a full assessment of a situation, rather than using AI as one of many inputs for human judgment. Middle managers will need skills to avoid such traps.

AI's Effect on Physician Performance

In a June 2023 study, AI working independently was found to be more effective at medical scan interpretation, diagnostic accuracy, and management reasoning than radiologists working with AI.[23]

Why is that? The study highlighted several biases the radiologists held against AI. They "often undervalued the AI input compared to their own judgment," sticking to their guns even when the AI model proved to be correct. But the AI models had their own distinctive flaws as well. AI agents were far less effective than humans at gathering patient information in initial consultations, frequently failing to ask follow-up questions and missing contextual clues.

While the report is damning about the effects of human biases, its major takeaway is not that human physicians should be replaced with "Robo Docs"; rather, it shows that AI is most effective when it is utilized in ways that take advantage of its own strengths *and* those of human doctors. Distrusting all of AI's outputs is folly, but so is accepting them all as gospel.

As AI tools provide "easy answers" to hard challenges, managers will need to be vigilant for "cognitive sloth"[24]—our natural preference for well-worn heuristics over mental exertion. Sure, the middle managers of the near future will spend less time ensuring compliance with organizational strategy, but they will spend more effort finding the right balance between originality and productivity.[25]

That is a key point. Leaders cannot be like students relying on ChatGPT to write term papers, or their critical thinking skills will atrophy, leaving them far worse off. AI *raises* the importance of excellent critical thinking rather than reducing it. Generative AI dazzles, but it rarely invents unprompted. Human beings must ask it the right questions and reject answers that are wrong or banal.

Human judgment will remain a vital ingredient in:

1. **Frontline creativity.** Every employee, not just the strategy team, must know when a canned answer is insufficient and how to frame a fresh question that pushes AI beyond the obvious.
2. **Managerial validation.** Middle managers will become quality-control nodes: comparing AI-generated recommendations with grounded truth and spotting mismatches, then intervening before small errors grow.
3. **Executive foresight.** Senior and middle leaders alike will have to look past the data's horizon, sensing faint tremors in customer sentiment, regulatory shifts, or stealth competitors that the models can't yet detect.

The revolution in middle management will drive far greater efficiency and speed. If organizations reconfigure processes and jobs, and equip people with the right skills, AI is an accelerator. If they fail to do so, AI merely automates yesterday's logic.

Consider, for instance, how AI revolutionizes the sales manager role.[26] Instead of spending hours digging through data looking for trends in their region, they can:

▸ Query AI using natural language and receive a report in seconds.
▸ Leverage customer data to better determine whom to reach, when, and with what messaging.
▸ Pose questions to their knowledge management platform to brush up on new offerings, significantly reducing ramp-up time.

Already, tools like Gong or Chorus provide automated analyses of sales calls, surfacing areas of improvement without manual call debriefs.

Tools like this change how teams coordinate. For managers, this means spending less time drilling teams on the company's twelve-step sales process, chasing documents and sign-offs, ensuring that implementation teams are looped in at the right steps, monitoring sales pipelines, tracking individual rep performances, and manually compiling forecasts.

For sales reps, it clears away a lot of the administrative work, like approving sales terms, that eat as much as two-thirds of their days. It means that managers (and their teams) can focus more time on sales and coaching. It frees time for them to collaborate with product teams, making better use of customer or prospect feedback on new offerings.

Plus, there is finally time to dedicate to strategic initiatives, like removing half of that twelve-step sales process and improving account assignments. The manager role won't go away. It will simply become more strategic and collaborative.

LEADING DECENTRALIZATION: FOUR GUARDRAILS FOR SENIOR EXECUTIVES

How can senior leaders ensure that decentralization meets all its goals? The figure shows four actions leaders should take in leading decentralization.

Over time, your expectations for frontline staff should continually rise. Some staff will leave or resist, but those who lean in will benefit from more meaningful, impactful, and higher value work.

The linchpin will be your managers. In the short term, it might be tempting to eliminate layers of middle management. As Mark Zuckerberg put it in a 2023 all-hands meeting at Meta, "I don't think you want a management structure that's just managers managing managers, managing managers, managing managers, managing the people who are doing the work."[27] It's hard to argue with that. Flatter, leaner hierarchies are already unlocking efficiency, but the right kind of management is increasingly vital. To get the most out of these new ways of working, the responsibilities and core skills of middle managers must evolve.

Leading Decentralization: Four Actions

Put Boundaries Around AI

- Specify which AI systems each team may use and the sanctioned use cases.
- Publish the list, invite suggestions, and revisit it quarterly.

Redefine "Manager"

- Shift middle managers from gatekeepers to "contributor-coaches." Grant day-to-day authority to the frontline team and use managers' expertise to vet AI outputs and unblock progress.
- Consider the training gaps managers must bridge to play this role.

Map Decision Lanes

- Draw clear routes for funding ideas, setting prices, and adjusting guardrails.
- Everyone should know who owns which call and when escalation is required.
- Leverage AI to make these guardrails searchable and explainable.

Hunt Blockers

- Charge managers with spotting the places where people have data but lack the right to act.
- Log these places, fix them fast, and track the reduction of these friction points as a core KPI.

A New Application of "Jobs to be Done"

Stephen's earlier book *Jobs to be Done: A Roadmap for Customer-Centered Innovation* expanded on a concept developed by his mentor Clayton Christensen, the Harvard Business School professor known also for theories such as Disruptive Innovation. The idea, in a nutshell, is that customers "hire" products to accomplish specific "Jobs" that arise in their lives. Understanding those Jobs well, you can shape offerings that are truly on target and don't overengineer expensive features. This concept doesn't just apply to customer choices; you can use it to optimize your company as well.

Take a fresh look at the internal Jobs that your organization needs to get done. What really needs to happen, and how can AI be leveraged to best help humans accomplish that? For instance, if one Job is to configure pricing to fit a customer's sweet spot, how might AI assess the customer's needs and their willingness to pay, balancing those against the underlying costs of serving that customer? How might humans ensure that the terms are appropriate and then sell the product to the customer? What might an AI-enabled process save in terms of time and labor versus your old ways of doing things? With this rethinking of the process, who would be doing what? What capabilities—AI and skill-based—would they require to succeed?

Microsoft is replacing its org charts with "work charts" focused on the work to be done, rather than on the seniority and supervisory authority of managers. You can do the same for each of your functions. Go through them systematically and specify all the Jobs within them, defining them not in terms of what humans currently do, but as discrete chunks of what must happen to keep the company running smoothly.

Could some of those Jobs be automated? Taken over by external partners? The answers could dramatically expand your possibilities.

CASE STUDY: Travelers' AI-Driven Knowledge

How are organizations utilizing AI to become nimbler and more distributed? By leveraging AI to bridge key knowledge gaps. Mojgan Lefebvre, chief technology and operations officer of Travelers Insurance, is empowering frontline staff to use AI, so that they own more day-to-day decision-making and work in ways that are both customer-centric and strategic.

Lefebvre and her team have concentrated some of their efforts on improving knowledge management, a common challenge for insurance companies. By leveraging generative AI and training large language models (LLMs) on specific domains, staff can synthesize specialized information, accelerating decision-making processes across the enterprise.

AI tools are already common in the insurance industry. Underwriters, for example, use them to assess aerial imagery and synthesize disaster risk data to evaluate properties remotely, sometimes beginning claims processes before families even know that their home was damaged.

As valuable as this reduction of time and expense is, Lefebvre has taken things a step further: "Our goal with AI deployment is not to use the technology as a cost cutting exercise," she says. "Rather, we have been focused for years on responsibly developing and differentiating AI capabilities across our three innovation priorities: extending our lead in risk expertise; providing great experiences for our customers, agents, brokers, and employees; and optimizing productivity and efficiency."

AI-driven knowledge management has other knock-on benefits as well. It allows underwriters and claims professionals to spend less time data crunching, document hunting, and sign-off chasing. Now they spend more time uncovering customer needs, collaborating with disparate teams, and shaping their internal and external communication to be clearer and more engaging. AI-driven knowledge management also empowers junior staff to take ownership of their career paths, expanding into subject areas in which they may not have much initial grounding. It enables octopus-like distributed intelligence.

The extent to which Travelers' knowledge management system anchors a more distributed and flexible organization depends upon the trustworthiness of its AI models. Ensuring this can be an expensive and costly endeavor, but Lefebvre sees it as critical. "This process is complex and requires careful attention from our teams," she states, "But it remains a key area of focus for us."

Afførd's Transition to Distributed Decision-Making

Let's revisit the furniture manufacturer we explored in Chapter 1. How does distributed intelligence change Afførd's day-to-day operations?

Historically, the company's massive scale and vertical integration meant that coordination had to be top-down, and consistent execution was paramount. The company could tightly control its sourcing, manufacturing, and distribution, so it did. But with the adoption of AI-enabled manufacturing and supply chain management, furniture parts are designed, built, and shipped faster than ever. Those parts can now also be customized, opening up an entirely new value proposition for customers—and a profit center for Afførd.

Afførd's working practices have adjusted to accommodate the use of AI. Machinery operators have been granted more autonomy to deal with time-sensitive mechanical failures and resource management. Supply-chain managers need fewer technical experts to crunch numbers. Instead, they coach their teams to read trends themselves and also to use AI's insights. Teams test options early, keeping goods moving smoothly.

Procurement staff no longer chase every contract. AI sets up and tracks routine deals. Freed from paperwork, teams build richer partnerships with suppliers. These ties unlock still more new options: fresh materials, advanced coatings, and work with renowned designers.

AI allows marketers to initiate and maintain millions of personalized conversations, both with people and with their bots. Teams spend far less time writing and launching campaigns and more time perfecting them.

Human labor still matters, but the skills that are needed are higher-level. Frontline employees and middle managers act with more freedom and face fewer approval layers. Collaborating with AI decision support tools, they deliver on tasks that demand judgment and strategic thinking.

Senior managers also play a different game. They spend less time picking products or store sites. Instead, they steer major shifts in strategy, help middle managers adapt, and work with AI to fine-tune the systems that power the business.

CHAPTER SUMMARY

Today, organizations need to be faster and more nimble to evolve and compete in a fast-changing world. They can't afford to allow decisions to be bottlenecked in centralized corporate cortexes.

To keep pace, companies must upgrade their "nervous systems" by giving decision-making power to the qualified people nearest each challenge and using AI to help teams gather facts, plan, decide, and act with greater speed and clarity. Middle managers need to change from control agents to coaches. Leaders must set clear AI boundaries and map decision rights, removing blockers and driving progress toward a more engaged and empowered workforce.

CHAPTER 3

Neural Necklace

*Unite knowledge, coordinate
innovation, and boost agility*

*"Octopuses proffer the possibility of a radically different form
of consciousness from what we are currently familiar with."*

—SIDNEY CARLS-DIAMANTE[28]

You wake up inside an unfamiliar body that is soft and boneless. Eight long limbs stir around you. A neural necklace—it links your other eight "brains," one in each limb, to each other. It's disorienting at first: Curious and impatient, each arm thinks for itself. You sense their chatter as faint electric murmurs, but they coordinate independently of you, sharing what they have done. They listen for your instinct but do not wait for your instructions. An itch of hunger flickers through you. Instantly, three arms launch forward, exploring a narrow, clear-walled tunnel in the rocks. You did not decide to do this; they moved the moment they felt your need. You're not sure if you're the pilot or the passenger.

Signals stream back from the sensors on your arms: left corridor dead-ends, right corridor leads to open water. You don't receive words, only sensations, but they are braided into a picture that your central brain translates into action. You tilt, funneling your bulbous head after the boldest arm. The others adjust automatically, a dance you conduct without conscious effort. Coordination emerges from conversation, not command.

Moments stretch; nerves hum. Finally, a leading arm breaches the water's surface, tasting cool air, and every neuron along the necklace flares with certainty. Two, three, four arms surge forward, snatch a small crab from a rock, and tug it back underwater in one fluid motion.

This is what it means to be intelligent everywhere. Insight radiates from the center, but discovery is coordinated at the edges—arms and head acting as one.

REWIRING YOUR ORGANIZATION'S BRAIN

Imagine an organization built the same way. Data flows like nerve signals and every team becomes an arm, free to sense, decide, and act, yet always in concert with the whole. That is the Octopus Organization: not a hierarchy of orders, but a living ballet of distributed insights, bound by a neural necklace—a distributed mind. With AI, you can weave that cord so that your enterprise can move as gracefully and adapt as quickly as the creature whose body you just inhabited.

As noted in Chapter 2, only a third of an octopus's neural tissue is in its central brain, where its executive functions like prioritization, memory, and visual analysis reside. The rest is in the nerve clusters that control its arms and the neural necklace that binds them together and coordinates them. Despite this, octopuses can recognize their handlers, navigate tricky mazes to access food, and may even have a rudimentary "theory of mind," the term that cognitive scientists use for the ability to recognize that other creatures have minds of their own.

This combination of "intelligence everywhere" and mission-specific focus is what happens in an organization when its data becomes truly transparent. Whether it is carefully tagged by humans or classified by AI, data can be acted on quickly and efficiently. This is not exactly artificial superintelligence (ASI) or even artificial general intelligence (AGI), but when it happens at scale it is super-human. The tools that empower this shift are already on the market, and they're having an impact.

In 2024, the popular messaging and collaboration platform Slack launched a suite of AI features that have helped users navigate endless message chains (essentially, resolving a problem Slack created in the first place). Reddit user "bbbaaahhhhh" (really) unpacks how Slack AI is changing the way his team collaborates and accesses information:

> Our team is geographically dispersed, and no one is con-sistently in the office, so Slack AI has clearly sped up the process for newer members to get answers to previously addressed questions without needing to wait to ask a human. . . .
>
> What we're finding is that our search metrics went down, and it's because people don't need to spend as much time digging around for what they're looking for. . . . [Before], we had so much noise coming at us all day, and it's helped reduce all those distractions.

Even simple AI search features can dramatically reduce the fric-tion that teams experience when pinpointing key information. These features are now standard on collaboration platforms like Microsoft 365, Notion, and Airtable. Of course, search is just the tip of the ice-berg. As we saw with Travelers, AI knowledge management systems can serve as powerful, organization-transforming sources of truth. Soon, AI assistants will act as executive assistants to every employee.

THE PENNY POST AND THE POWER OF DEMOCRATIZED DATA

For most of history, mail was a service provided exclusively to the wealthy, delivered at great expense. Messengers were highly paid lest they be tempted to steal the goods they were carrying or to sell the information. That was true until 1680, when the merchant William Dockwra developed the Penny Post, a system through which pre-paid letters could be dropped off at hundreds of receiving offices and delivered anywhere in London on the same day.

Within a year, the system had greatly democratized written communication. A maidservant could scribble a note to her mother two districts away and receive an answer the same day. Shopkeepers could post orders to suppliers and bills to customers, confident that they'd be received and acted upon in hours instead of days or weeks. Within a couple of years, London was bound together by a web of ink and paper and stamps. It was as if the city had become a creature whose arms had suddenly awakened an ability to communicate with each other. In a similar way, organizations that utilize AI to democratize the curation and synthesis of information will dramatically reduce the friction of internal and external collaboration.

Recently, Jonathan used an AI tool to customize a mass-mailing to promote his new video. Each email included a comment based on his previous interactions with the recipient, and a reason, based on their job descriptions, that his newest video would be relevant to them. It also included personalized content based on public information about their company. This is what happens when data flows freely.

As networks expand internally and externally, it's critical that data stem from a variety of contexts and that it's accessible and actionable to all who need it. AI is getting better at structuring unstructured data. It increasingly acts as the "telephone operator" for companies, determining what is important to share, making it easily findable, and providing guidance on how to act on it. The power of free-flowing information extends beyond an organization's inner workings; it also improves its ability to coordinate with its network of external partners.

Agentic AI—which goes beyond analyzing and synthesizing information to directly implementing its own recommendations—radically speeds the cycle from sensing to interpretation to action.

At the same time, AI enables massive scale by automating so many functions. In doing so, it reduces the coordination costs that economist Ronald Coase famously cited as the key factor that limits the size of firms: "A firm will tend to expand until the costs of organizing an extra transaction within the firm become equal to the costs of carrying out the same transaction by means of an exchange on the open market."[29]

Coase also argued that "transaction costs" are what led to the existence of firms in the first place, because transacting with outside partners for economic activities creates administrative burdens and inefficiencies. When Coase wrote *The Nature of the Firm* back in 1937, the costs of those transactions were substantial. It was inconceivable that an organization might have tens of thousands of contractors (as an on-demand labor platform like Upwork now provides) or millions of vendors (as Amazon now offers). Today, there is still a little friction in dealing with new contractors or vendors, but transaction costs have been rapidly declining as information systems improve and align.

AI will put this trend on steroids. While firms might grow to be very large (like Amazon), because they can coordinate so much more seamlessly with webs of partners, they might also become very small.

Attend to Your Ecosystem

One thing we know from nature is that the health of ecosystems matters as much as the robustness of their individual components. Though the octopus survived the sudden collapse of the Mesozoic ecosystem, three-quarters of the species on the planet did not. The global business ecosystem is going through a similarly massive shift today, and AI can help companies manage the disruption.

The Trade Desk is an AI-powered ad platform that helps digital advertisers target consumers across multiple devices, channels, and markets. Every time someone visits a partner's website or advances to a new page in a mobile app, Trade Desk can match the visitor with a colection from its vast inventory of ads, homing in on the right one to show the right person at the right time.

Since Trade Desk depends on its ecosystem of partners—brands, ad agencies, websites, and mobile applications—to meet its objectives, it is attentive to all their needs, including those of partners' human employees. It invests heavily in training and user events for partners' line workers and in reporting systems for their leaders. It calculates the value created by partners' ads, counsels them on best practices, and keeps them up to date on critical trends in the marketplace. Trade Desk is AI-infused, but it recognizes that its business partners are people who need human attention.

AVOIDING THE PITFALLS OF FRICTIONLESS INFORMATION

Just because you can collect and distribute data doesn't mean you should. Most employees don't need to know their colleagues' salaries, for example. Data transparency costs more than it delivers if the data isn't used in the right way. Employees don't want to feel as if their every keystroke is monitored. They may also balk at the additional administrative lift that collecting and sharing certain metrics imposes on them, such as delivering constant project status updates.

Much of the important information leaders require to make key decisions can't be measured. Data collection and distribution involves judgment calls. It's easy to mistake a proxy for the thing it's being used to measure. For instance, tracking keystrokes and mouse movements is used to measure call center productivity. This KPI incentivizes employees to conduct busywork that produces more keystrokes, when they could be using the time to find better solutions for customers. Efficiency metrics often discourage employees from seeking advice from experienced managers, leaders, and contributors, whose stories may be unknown to AI.

That said, AI systems are only as good as the data they process— if too much data is suppressed, they can't do their jobs well. Whatever you do, prevent the mantra "Measure What Matters" from turning into "Only What Can be Measured Matters."

Peter Drucker famously said, "What gets measured gets done." But are you measuring the right things? If you're not, AI may confidently encourage you to make the wrong investments and draw the wrong conclusions. During the Vietnam War, the Pentagon collected reams of data on how many enemy soldiers were killed, yet the clear qualitative trend was that the US was losing the war. To win in a world where so much is measurable, it's important to be clear on what matters and prioritize that.

Log off your computer and ask yourself this question: Does your map match the reality on the ground?

PREPARING STAFF FOR THE DATA DELUGE

As your people gain access to more information, their ability to efficiently and accurately assess it will become dramatically more important. Unless organizations invest in this skill, data transparency can cost more in labor than it provides in accuracy.

Two gremlins are especially liable to gum up the works: groupthink and "analysis paralysis."

- Groupthink occurs when organizations use data to create and sustain consensus rather than to form new insights.
- Analysis paralysis is an anxiety about making decisions without having absolutely every variable pinned down.

Here are a few ways to inoculate your teams against these gremlins.

Godzilla vs. the Newt

The more organizations rely on AI for strategic decision-making, the more important it will be for decision-makers to hear "unreasonable" points of view. One fun way to nurture out-of-the-box perspectives is to ask what would make a challenge dramatically larger or smaller. We aren't wrestling an alligator, it's a Komodo dragon. What would be even bigger—a T. rex? No, bigger—Godzilla. Now, what would make it smaller, an iguana? No smaller—a newt. Force extreme thinking before you gravitate back toward the center. Diverge before you converge.

TRIZ

Genrich Altshuller was an underappreciated genius—so underappreciated that he was prosecuted for "innovator's sabotage" and sent to a gulag by Stalin! After Stalin died and Altshuller was released, he published his *Theory of Inventive Problem Solving*—TRIZ, in its Russian acronym—which was a real gift to innovators. It was typically Soviet: mathy, statistical, and inordinately complex. In short, it was unworkable for pretty much any human but its inventor. But AI has no such limits. Introduce your AI to TRIZ, give it your data, and set it loose to brainstorm solutions. It will come up with approaches that neither you nor any other human could have imagined.

Risk Bands

Leaders who create and specify "risk bands"—the upper and lower bounds of anticipated risks—give teams permission to ask challenging questions and experiment with untested ideas. By making room for constructive dissent, they expose overlooked insights and spark new directions for innovation.

We can see clear evidence for this in . . . playgrounds. In a telling experiment, a team of landscape architects probed how playground fencing impacted the way children play. In playgrounds with fences, kids used the full space available, frequently playing near the fence as well as at the center. When there wasn't a fence, they stuck close to the main equipment like the slide and swings.[30] Make sure that your teams feel safe to explore their whole playgrounds.

Haim's Law

Haim Mendelson, a famed teacher of critical thinking at the Stanford Graduate School of Business, insists that most of the time he doesn't need to even look at the data to judge whether a student's business plan is bad. He just works through the logic. Often, more data won't replace critical thinking. AI can help you with critical thinking, and it can check for cognitive biases, something most humans have trouble doing for themselves.

Let the Devil Have an Advocate

Within the Israeli Military Intelligence Directorate sits a tiny team called the Devil's Advocate Unit. The unit's role is to vet and challenge intelligence assumptions and products. This behavior can also be baked into AI models. Rather than optimizing AI for the safest and most predictable answers, you can configure it to suggest high-variance and unorthodox options, or to push against your assumptions.

Door 1 vs. Door 2

Leaders often fall into the trap of overanalyzing a decision, prospecting for a golden insight rather than making the hard call. When faced with a choice between Door 1 and Door 2, your job as a leader in the AI Age will be to determine when you have "enough" data to act with a reasonable expectation of success. It's not to prove a grand unified theory. When speed is more important than being right, move fast.

CASE STUDY: **Amazon's Focus on Open Interfaces**

In its first twenty years, Amazon grew extraordinarily quickly while keeping its teams small and close-knit. Each team built modular solutions that fit in a plug-and-play manner with those from other teams (as prescribed in Amazon's well-known 2002 "API mandate").[31] This way of working prevented (and still prevents) the organization from developing silos. All teams share data and communicate with each other via "service interfaces." No other form of inter-process data and software communication is allowed: no direct linking, no direct reads of other teams' data, no shared-memory models, no back doors. Those service interfaces were designed to be exposed to developers outside of the company. Building code in interchangeable blocks linked by interfaces allows Amazon to mix and match solutions in different ways. Even hyper-specific solutions can be adapted to solve problems in other parts of the organization.

Underpinning this system is a form of open code documentation that allows teams to understand what the others are developing, reducing duplicate work and encouraging teams to work on problems together. The modularity and transparency allow Amazon to gain the benefits of scale while avoiding its inefficiencies.

Now Amazon is leveraging its development system to launch AI applications quickly in ways that target key customer needs. As a leader at AWS put it to us, "find that specific use case, work backwards . . . [and] scale from there." With its modular form of software development, reliance on small teams, and overarching focus on data consolidation, Amazon is as resilient and nearly as nimble with 1.5 million employees as when it was a startup.

Afførd Connects the Dots

Life at Afførd used to occur in silos. Product formulated the year's offerings, Operations tooled up to manufacture them, Marketing sold them, and so on. Management reviewed umpteen spreadsheets and slides as data and plans were passed from silo to silo, and then up and down the managerial pyramid.

Now, Afførd's managers don't even have to query their systems for information. Much like *Bloomberg* or *The Wall Street Journal*, AI provides a continuous dashboard of the most important information of the day. Managers can query the system for more in-depth data, but the reporting is so good that few do.

The dashboard provides hourly updates on production forecasts and allows managers to drill down to better understand the configurations of machinery and labor that AI has determined are optimal. The Marketing department in Mexico can see what's been most effective in selling similar products in Spain and Colombia. When quality issues emerge, it's easy to find the machine operators, even if they're on the other side of the world, and ask them what's going on. Universal translators allow for seamless communication. Information doesn't just flow seamlessly. AI proactively sends insight where it is most useful.

These developments haven't supplanted critical thinking. In fact, top-quality inquiry is more valuable than ever. Managers need to assess whether they're really seeing the most pertinent data. They spend less time on reporting and more on coming up with creative ways to apply their insights. Because they spend less time obtaining and ingesting data, they focus more on making the best use of it.

CHAPTER SUMMARY

Organizations that balance "intelligence everywhere" with a mission-specific focus are far more flexible, resilient, and efficient than those that either centralize or completely devolve decision-making authority. AI communication and data-sharing tools reduce the friction of internal and external collaboration. Acting as a "neural necklace," they enable fast, localized decision-making by democratizing access to information and providing a "single source of truth." With these tools, teams can become modular, responding more quickly to changes in their markets and driving local decision-making.

But frictionless information has its pitfalls. Be wary of the dangers of groupthink, developing an overreliance on measurable outputs, and succumbing to analysis paralysis. Leaders must encourage dissent and human judgment. While AI should be configured to explore unconventional ideas, managers must resist the temptation to outsource human intellect. It's their job to ensure the opposite: that AI is a catalyst for distributed creativity, faster learning, and more rigorous decision-making.

CHAPTER 4

Three Hearts

*Adapt to shifting needs with the
right leadership toolkit*

*"What kind of god gives a cephalopod
three but a human only one?"*

**—JOY SULLIVAN,
"AN OCTOPUS HAS THREE WHOLE HEARTS" (POEM)**

An octopus hovers above a coral reef. Inside its body are three hearts: a systemic engine that drives blood throughout its body and two branchial pumps that serve its gills.

A faint chemical trace brushes an arm: Shark! Instantly, the octopus's pigment cells flash coral-red hues. As the shark lunges, the octopus performs a feat that no mammal can survive: It gives itself a heart attack. Its systemic heart shuts off as its branchial pair surges, flooding its brain and limbs with oxygen. Then the octopus's siphon erupts, rocketing the creature forward while a black ink plume clouds the shark's view. One arm flicks to steer, another tastes the current for signs of potential cover, a third skims the sand to navigate its escape route, all of them improvising without getting in each other's way.

Forty body-lengths away, the octopus's systemic heart restarts and its skin color reverts to its usual mottled grey. As it regains its senses, the octopus considers where it should get its next meal.

THREE HEARTS, THREE MANAGEMENT SYSTEMS

Too many organizations rely on rigid processes and architecture. This stems from an assumption of the railroad age: that most people lack the knowledge they need to improvise sound strategic decisions.

In the world of AI, that is no longer true. We aren't putting AI on the org chart, we are replacing it.

AI-oriented leaders of Octopus Organizations don't depend on a rigid "line and staff" organization model in which key directives flow from the top down. Instead, they shift between three management styles, depending on the context. Each corresponds to one of the octopus's three hearts:

- ▸ **Analytic Heart.** Pause, assess data, decide with precision.
- ▸ **Agile Heart.** Deliver rapid bursts of action at the edge.
- ▸ **Aligned Heart.** Keep culture and purpose beating in sync with the organization's actions.

Each heart corresponds to a distinct management process paired with a complementary leadership style. When these functions work together seamlessly, they make organizations nimble and ready to navigate a dynamic, unpredictable environment. Survival hinges on the ability to toggle—to disengage the big Analytic Heart when necessary, surge the edge pumps, and keep those engines beating in rhythm. Every enterprise needs that triple cadence.

The Analytic and Agile Hearts need to be kept in balance. Organizations can err toward either extreme. A large organization that Stephen works with proudly boasts of its flat, cell-like structure in which employees lack titles and there is no formal hierarchy. This creates speed and responsiveness, but it's often unclear who should make the hard calls. This greatly impedes the organization's ability to make big decisions. Leaders need to use the right heart for the right purpose, just like the octopus does.

ANALYTIC HEART

You are five minutes late for your Zoom meeting with your consultant—not someone from Accenture, but a virtual avatar that has all of your knowledge as well as all of your firm's. It searches its databases, including transcripts from Zoom meetings, market research, and analyst calls. It can help you think through the right frameworks to make the best decisions. And it doesn't mind you being late—this consultant works 24/7 without ever complaining.

Note that the AI is your consultant, not your replacement. AI may (and should) advise you, but the decisions are yours. Should you double down on what's working now or invest in a new venture? What balance should you strike between short- and long-term bets?

Questions like these involve goal setting, value judgments, and hard-to-quantify risks. AI can help you make the right call, but it will be quite some time before it navigates all the ambiguities and hard decisions on its own.

Many other management questions are less opaque and simply require that the executive:

- ▸ Has contextual awareness of the organization and its environment
- ▸ Exercises sound judgment
- ▸ Makes decisions that nest into a larger set of actions

While these skills take years to train into staff, AI is fast becoming quite good at them. In many cases, AI is better than humans. It will change the way you lead, but it won't just be your job that changes. AI tools will collaborate with your most junior people, too, making them capable of much more complex decision-making.

So, what's a senior leader to do? When goals are ambiguous and systemic impacts are difficult to assess, leaders must keep decision rights to themselves or collaborate with AI tools to find boundaries. Decisions with definable risk bands should be devolved to staff and AI.

Increasingly, management will shift from product to process quality control—ensuring that staff is leveraging the right data and asking software the right questions. AI isn't perfect, but it is persuasive, so employees' critical thinking and gut instincts must be sharper than ever. AI requires human genius as much as humans need AI tools.

AGILE HEART

As Columbia Business School's Rita McGrath warns, leaders too often mistake "untested assumptions . . . [for] fact."[32] Instead of experimenting or systematically weighing their options, she adds, "it's much more of a 'we're going to assume we know and damn the torpedoes, full speed ahead.'" The Agile Heart is a flexible leadership style that provides psychological safety to frontline staff, freeing them to experiment and build, while enabling middle and senior management to vet and track experiments.

L'Oréal provides a shining example of the ways that AI tools and agile leadership combine to drive results. The consumer packaged goods industry is highly sensitive to trends, not to mention inflation, supply chain disruptions, and an uncertain tariff landscape.[33] L'Oreal leverages AI to continually analyze and respond to customer needs.

TrendSpotter, one of its market analysis tools, continuously scrapes and analyzes data from billions of online sources, including social media platforms, blogs, and video content, using natural language processing (NLP) and image recognition algorithms that were trained on multilingual datasets from across L'Oreal's global footprint.

On the product development side, L'Oréal integrates AI into R&D workflows through systems like ModiFace. Originally developed for virtual try-on applications, L'Oreal's chemists use it to simulate ingredient combinations and skin profiles.

L'Oreal's data-to-product pipeline is significantly faster and more precise than traditional methods. But the innovation systems don't just encompass IT. L'Oreal's leadership empowers its staff to iterate quickly without layers of central approval, allowing their teams to be the first to address specific market needs or changes in consumer behaviors. The results can be astonishing. L'Oreal has been able to move from concept to product-on-shelf in as little as *six weeks.*

How well can your middle managers spot threats, assess potential innovations, and incubate them into opportunities? Doing these things well entails the following:

1. **Effective trend-sensing.** Like L'Oréal, use social listening tools and an empowered "edge" to get ahead of market changes.
2. **Venture capital–like assessment of potential opportunities and threats.** Encourage a high degree of risk tolerance, emphasizing scalable ventures over guaranteed returns. Empower middle managers to treat new opportunities as speculative but testable bets, without fear of reprisal when there is a failed experiment.
3. **A portfolio strategy, with distributed teams each working on independent concepts.** Think asymmetrically about wins and losses, assuming that 90 percent of new product and service ideas will ultimately fail. Work with AI decision support tools to allocate resources based on continuous assessment of each concept's viability.
4. **A structure for learning, in an apolitical fashion, from successes and failures.** Establish metrics that allow your teams to assess whether a concept has failed. Cut your losses early and conduct postmortems so lessons learned can be incorporated into future experiments. Crucially, document what you have done!
5. **Double down quickly on the opportunities that are most promising.** When it comes to scaling concepts, avoid a scattershot approach. Anticipate few unicorns, but when you find them, leverage them aggressively.

Ideally, capabilities 1 through 4 should be almost entirely independent from senior leadership.

In addition to its value in handling disruptions, agility and flexibility will become essential in your core business. After years of hype, marketing to individuals is finally practical—and so are other ultra-targeted tactics that once seemed impossible.

Walmart's Scintilla Platform: Powering Agility Through Merchant-Supplier Collaboration

Established by Walmart Data Ventures, Scintilla leverages AI to integrate real-time supply chain data, online and in-person customer touchpoints, and external market trends. This powerful end-to-end analytics platform delivers insight to both Walmart and its suppliers.

When international trade policies shift, product costs change rapidly and availability shrivels up. Scintilla minimizes disruption by delivering timely insights on sourcing alternatives, cost impacts, and inventory adjustments. This lets Walmart quickly reroute shipments and alter vendor contracts. Suppliers, in turn, gain visibility into Walmart's evolving needs, allowing for synchronized adjustments to production and distribution plans.

Through predictive analytics, the platform identifies emerging trends in customer behavior, from seasonal changes to lifestyle-driven preferences. Walmart and its suppliers use these insights to optimize assortment, pricing, and promotions. The platform's In-Home Usage Tests service allows subscribers to conduct research with verified Walmart customers, delivering insights into how they use products in real-world settings.

Ultimately Scintilla does more than help Walmart and its external partners become more agile—it deepens their collaboration.

ALIGNED HEART

The Aligned Heart ensures that—amid the hyperspeed of business in the AI Age—the organization's culture and purpose remain guiding forces and motivating to employees. This is more critical now than ever. You may find yourself guiding your people through a valley of despair. Let's be clear about the challenge: AI adoption will disrupt how staff relate to their roles and responsibilities, potentially sapping their motivation and diminishing their satisfaction.

In a 2025 study, researchers from Zhejiang University examined how collaborations with generative AI impacted worker psychology. They found a clear trade-off. While tasks were completed more quickly and effectively with AI, workers' intrinsic motivations were "undermined," even after AI supports were removed.[34] AI led people to feel bored or disengaged by their work.

At a macro level, we see signs that AI usage correlates with declines in worker satisfaction. A 2025 economic analysis from researchers at Emory University used Glassdoor reviews from employees to gauge satisfaction in high AI exposure versus low AI exposure jobs, across occupations. They saw a relation between higher AI exposure, lower job satisfaction, and poorer work-life balance ratings.[35] This isn't to say that AI is inherently detrimental to worker satisfaction, but it does suggest that some of the ways AI tools are adopted may need to change. To overcome employee resistance, lean into your role as a culture setter, exemplify your organization's values, and encourage employees to buy into their purpose.

As Jordi Canals of IESE notes, senior managers in AI-enabled enterprises must prioritize "vision, values, determination, passion, consistency and creativity" over operations.[36] Alex Adamopoulos, founder and CEO of Emergn, emphasizes how important it is for leaders to have a clear, yet non-quantifiable, sense of what "great" means for the organization, "When organizations are about to take on a transformation program . . . we encourage people to answer one important question: what does 'great' look like? 'Great' is not only outcomes-based. 'Great' is emotional. The 'great' conversation matters because it helps an organization decide if they really do believe what their purpose is."[37]

Defining a shared sense of purpose will become critical for leaders, because far from sidelining humans, use of AI requires your people to be more human than ever. AI will automate the things that can be automated, but leaders will need people to do the things AI can't.

Don't Treat People Like Robots

The Aligned Heart uses human intuition and empathy to:

- ▶ **Understand what people need.** AI promises efficiency and precision, but it stumbles when confronted with the murky depths of group dynamics. Only human leaders can face anger and discontent, hear out grievances, and build trust. Doing so requires sensitivity to human emotions and social interactions that no algorithm can replicate.

- ▶ **Respond to unpredictability.** AI excels where there is an abundance of data, but when faced with uncertainty and data scarcity, its strengths become limitations. Decisiveness and responsiveness in the face of unpredictability are human qualities. Remember, data is inherently about the past. As useful as it is as a starting point for predictions, humans must retain the flexibility to adapt when reality deviates from your own or AI's extrapolations.

- ▶ **Inspire others.** Let's not give AI too much credit. Generative AI tools are typically designed to find the most likely answer, not the best answer. Humans excel at imagining possibilities and rallying others to pursue them.

AI demands leadership, and it is leaders who lead. AI does not.

Don't Give People Robot Jobs

Your role as a culture setter should be clear, but what practical steps can you take to protect and enhance your people's job satisfaction? We have a few recommendations:

1. **Frame AI as an *augmentation*, not a replacement for meaningful work.** AI tools can handle repetitive, unsafe, or

low-autonomy tasks and enhance work that involves human interaction, creativity, and judgment, but they should never be framed as "replacements" for human workers. Understand what workers find most fulfilling about their jobs and protect that from "AI outsourcing."

2. **Encourage (and invest in) continuous learning and AI skill development.** Fear of obsolescence is a key driver of worker dissatisfaction with AI, so frame AI as more of an opportunity than a threat. Support employees as they develop AI literacy, emphasizing how AI skills open up mobility within your organization. Double down on training strategic judgment and communication skills. Remember that these will become vital for early career employees who need to make more complex decisions than ever.

3. **Foster psychological safety and transparent communication.** AI adoption should involve dialogue between leadership and frontline staff. Encourage feedback and involvement from employees when designing, testing, and implementing AI tools. Openly address their fears about AI and job security, highlighting how AI will shift work in more meaningful directions.

4. **Continuously measure impact.** Regularly assess job satisfaction, stress levels, and AI-related concerns. A pre-adoption baseline should be compared with follow-up surveys within the first few months of rollout and then again at about the six-to-nine-month mark, while actively addressing staff issues.

AI adoption is more than just another tech rollout. It's a change management process. If you don't explicitly acknowledge and address the ways that AI affects job satisfaction and purpose, it can easily lead to a less engaged and less motivated workforce. As a change maker and culture setter, it is up to you to ensure that your workforce sees AI as a necessary and organic part of a larger organizational story, not an interloper.

CASE STUDY: **A Global Leader Takes Multiple Approaches for Managing Medical Research**

Healthcare organizations tend to be risk-averse and procedures-based, whether their specialty is high-risk neurosurgery or routine checkups. Most of their leaders prioritize Analytic Hearts, and for good reasons. But processes that minimize risk may not be well suited for researchers who are pursuing breakthroughs.

Mass General Brigham (MGB), a premier health system in New England and one of the largest medical research centers in the world, successfully balances its Analytic, Agile, and Aligned Hearts in managing its renowned research programs. The organization blends top-down and bottom-up systems that provide structure where needed while simultaneously encouraging collaborations across the organization and empowering staff to commercialize their findings.

Much of MGB's primary medical research occurs within "cores," established Centers of Excellence in which researchers study specific diseases, conditions, and treatments. Cores bring subject matter experts together and help MGB share indirect costs. At the same time, the model improves the chances of winning external grants. A Clinical Trials Office also systematizes the development, negotiation, and execution of industry-sponsored clinical research. Together, these structures smooth out risks, maximize funding, and reduce the costs of innovation. They are the Analytic Heart in action.

But MGB also empowers its researchers and clinicians to find innovative ways of translating their research into medical treatments and solutions—the Agile Heart. Mass General Brigham Innovation, an internal commercialization team, provides training and resources to help innovators file patents and identify potential investors. Its Innovator MESH Network is an online portal that facilitates connections among clinicians, researchers, co-founders, and investors.

Another group, Mass General Brigham Ventures, collaborates with partners to invest in early-stage life science startups based on intellectual property created within MGB's research community. Mixing the benefits of open innovation and an internal venture fund, these programs help researchers and clinicians connect, collaborate, and commercialize their discoveries without following a strictly linear process.

Finally, MGB's Digital Clinical Research Organization helps industry partners develop and launch Software as a Medical Device products. Companies large and small work with the AI CRO to refine algorithms, gain advice on deployment and clinical integration, and validate and achieve regulatory clearance for new tools. The program helps ensure that AI is being used in ways that are clinically relevant and impactful for patients.

Driving the effort to integrate Mass General Brigham's clinical, academic, and commercial services is its President and CEO Anne Klibanski, who is the personification of the Aligned Heart. Under her leadership, for instance, MGB launched "For Every Patient," a commitment to "deliver high-quality, personalized care rooted in equity."[38] She also refers to MGB's more than two hundred years of history to reinforce its core principles and long-term thinking.

Chief Strategy Officer Andy Shin also sees possibilities for broadening Agile Heart leadership across MGB while strengthening its Aligned Heart. Leveraging recent work from a system-wide task force focused on improving the well-being and experience of its staff, MGB has piloted AI assistants for primary care physicians (PCPs). The assistants transcribe notes, fill in electronic health records, flag relevant family history, and keep track of patient preferences that might easily be missed, allowing PCPs to shift their focus toward deeper patient interactions.

As he put it to us:

This is a common refrain you'll hear from PCPs: "I'm either a human or a robot." They're stuck in this place where they are asked to perform automation-like behaviors, where they need to be consistent and fit in all of this data so we can coordinate care into the tools that we have.

What AI has been able to do is to handle a lot of the data entry for PCPs, but it goes beyond that. AI assistants aren't just there to reconcile information. They actually go beyond what humans can do, consolidating voluminous patient data and making important connections that can help the PCP tailor their care.[39]

With AI, PCPs are not only freed to refocus on the "human" components of their roles. AI empowers them to take more decisive action in the moment by drawing insights from disparate information in an accessible way.

MGB's programs balance deliberate outcomes with individual autonomy, all while working toward a common set of commitments that bind the disparate arms of the organization. In doing so, it uses all three hearts.

Afførd Moves Beyond the Analytic Heart

In managing its traditionally top-down organization, Afførd's leadership team prioritized the Analytic Heart. They focused on limiting risks, controlling the consistency of outputs, and ensuring that all the pieces of their vertically integrated system meshed. Agility and Alignment were less important.

AI changed the picture. Internal innovation exploded when the company's inventory of customizable parts and furniture styles became usable by its expanding list of external collaborators. With manufacturing and procurement simplified, Afførd teams are now exploring new design services. The company has piloted design partnerships with several commercial real estate firms and co working spaces.

As the old advantages of scale and integration ebbed, new startups sprang up to challenge traditional incumbents. Afførd has kept those new entrants at bay with its similarly Agile Heart style of management. Sometimes it even funds, produces, and distributes goods for these entities.

Those big shifts require new Aligned Heart skills. New, more flexible forms of working didn't initially gel with all teams. Some workers had honed their crafts over decades and chafed at the idea that they were at risk of becoming redundant.

Afførd's leadership recognized and acknowledged that, and they did what they could to help by providing generous severance and outplacement services for those whose jobs really did become obsolete. They invested heavily in retraining for those whose new job descriptions required it. Leadership also highlighted the upside of becoming a company where every worker would have more autonomy and more voice in the company's day-to-day operations.

Yes, some forms of work needed to change, but Afførd committed to delivering on its promise of high-quality goods, sustainably made, at competitive prices. Its ways of working had shifted, but the company's core values hadn't.

CHAPTER SUMMARY

In volatile environments, leaders cannot stick to one rigid management style. Instead, they must shift between three different styles to suit a variety of challenges. The Analytic Heart emphasizes data-driven decision-making, the Agile Heart supports rapid experimentation and frontline autonomy, and the Aligned Heart ensures cultural cohesion and purpose.

CHAPTER 5

RNA-Powered Resilience

Accelerate action and frontline innovation through accurate sensing

*"Not just skin but script it bends,
octopus edits where survival depends."*

—CHATGPT

Warm water slides over the reef when, suddenly, an upwelling of cold current surges from the deep. A hunting octopus feels its muscles go heavy in mid-lunge, as if time itself has thickened. Its neurons fire more slowly in the cold; the fish it was chasing swims away.

Inside the octopus's body, a silent rescue attempt unfolds. Millions of newly minted messenger RNA strands are seized by ADAR enzymes, the octopus's molecular editors, which tweak the makeup of certain proteins, acclimating them to colder temperatures.[40] Within hours, new cold-water proteins replace the sluggish originals; the octopus's arms regain their snap, and the hunt resumes as though nothing had happened.

SHIFTING FROM DNA TO RNA

When most organizations hit a sudden new current (a rate shock, a demand crash, an onerous regulation), they freeze, trim their activities, and wait for the climate to improve. Like the ancient ammonites, they falter because their operational "DNA" is too fixed to cope with rapid change.

Octopus Organizations reprogram their processes and structures. This goes beyond fluid communication or decentralized control. Much as the octopus rewrites its RNA to fine-tune its survival mechanisms, Octopus Organizations transform their cores from within.

Like the octopus, the Octopus Organization is continuously sensing and reconfiguring; always looking for early signals and adapting before change hits its bottom line. Adaptation is a continual process, not a fixed destination. While senior leaders maintain a dashboard of activities, Octopus Organizations put new processes into production and retire old ones with only minor direction—long before customers or financial statements feel the chill.

The octopus doesn't convene a committee; it edits the active transcript before its precious time (and oxygen) run out. In the pages ahead, we'll show you how to embed the same capacity in your organization, turning AI assistants, modular processes, and middle-manager "editors" into a living RNA layer that can recode strategy on the fly.

Survival in the AI Age won't hinge on rigid master plans that are handed down from above. It will depend on how quickly you can adapt.

ACCELERATING YOUR RNA REQUIRES INTENTIONALLY EVOLVING YOUR DNA

One of the great learnings from the Covid crisis was how poorly prepared most governments were for the disruptions it unleashed. Though public health measures, vaccines, and advanced medicine had made pandemics less frequent and devastating than they once were, viruses are notoriously adaptable. Far from historical anomalies, mass contagions are facts of modern, interconnected societies—the more modern and interconnected, the more inevitable. You would have thought the recent SARS and Ebola scares would have better prepared governments for "the big one."[41]

As risk averse and strategically oriented as big corporations tend to be, most were just as blindsided by the virus as the world's governments were. Eight of America's ten largest publicly traded companies failed to even mention global pandemics as a material risk in their pre-2020 SEC filings. When the shutdowns began, few had a Plan B on hand.

The pandemic hit hard. Yet many of its worst effects stemmed from long-standing problems that leaders had ignored. Short-term thinking and fragile global supply chains were clear risks that could have been fixed.

Companies that knew what to look for and took the initiative on what they saw provided powerful demonstrations of *wei-ji*, a Chinese portmanteau for crisis—danger (*wei*) and opportunity (*ji*). In crisis is the possibility of upside for the prepared.

Consider Amazon. It supplied its customers with products that other retailers couldn't. It thought big and deployed its own ships, docking them at ports on the East Coast, which were less backed up than the Port of Los Angeles. All the way back in 2016, Amazon had applied for a license to become its own freight forwarder. While its competitors were paralyzed by a shortage of shipping containers, it started manufacturing its own. By the end of the *annus horribilis* of 2020, Amazon's net profits had risen 84 percent.

Toyota became the biggest automobile maker in the world during the pandemic because of two key capabilities. It had already designed its operations for maximum flexibility, so it was able to rapidly retool its production lines to make delivery trucks, instead of minivans, when demand shifted. Toyota also maintained stockpiles of components that came from single, potentially vulnerable sources.

That second capability wasn't a result of supernatural foresight; it was a pragmatic response to a costly failure. During the Fukushima nuclear disaster in 2011, Toyota had to shut down production because it lacked access to components that were manufactured there. To guard against future disruptions, it maintained six-month stockpiles of 250 key components.

Like octopuses, Amazon and Toyota were champions of adaptability. With the help of AI, your organization can be one too. We live in a volatile era. If leaders want to continue creating value, they'll need to improve two capabilities that have been neglected in recent years: resilience and foresight.

THE POWER OF SUPER SENSING

As great a disruptor as AI will be, it also enables the resilience and prescience that can turn disruption into opportunity. The precondition for doing so is *sensing*.

Like the octopus, which uses its roughly 2,000 suction cups to smell the water for predators and prey, Octopus Organizations use AI to create 360-degree maps of their external and internal environments. They collect and analyze massive amounts of data to reveal structures within the seemingly unstructured. They surface problems before they metastasize, and they identify opportunities to drive greater efficiencies or create new products.

The human element is more critical than ever. To identify threats and opportunities, leaders need to recognize both the positive and negative implications of the many "what-ifs" surrounding them.

For instance, how will the collision of financial, operational, external, and strategic issues impact your business? How might inflation, supply chain disruptions, and a nationwide cyberattack combine to impact you?

While the exact future is often a surprise, it's often possible to know the range of possibilities and how long you have to react. A strong intelligence capability increases the prescience and precision of your responses.

WHAT'S MORE VALUABLE THAN DATA? CUSTOMER INTIMACY

Sensing is one thing. Understanding is another. While the world swirls around us, your customers' priorities—their "Jobs to be Done"[42]—are unlikely to change fast. Understanding those priorities deeply can be your North Star during even accelerating change.

For example, Procter & Gamble (P&G) uses AI to both manage its supply chain and stay closer to its customers. When customer insights are needed—say, from a person doing laundry in Delhi—AI instantly creates a synthetic consumer for marketers to interview. At the same time, P&G constantly surveys real consumers and interviews them in-depth, as real people can tell you things that AI bots can't. For instance, P&G found that a leading Job to be Done for users of premium laundry detergents is a deeply human one—to feel like they're being a good parent.

Moreover, P&G widely trains its staff to recognize and respond to consumer needs. While there are many insights professionals in the organization, consumer understanding is not kept within some high priesthood of the specially anointed. People throughout brand teams understand how to interpret insights data, so the democratization of insights throughout the organization can translate into corresponding actions.

One powerful way to use AI is to help organizations understand what knowledge we do and don't have. It can help by categorizing factors into four groups:

- ▶ Known Knowns (things that are fairly certain to happen)
- ▶ Known Unknowns (things you know you can uncover but haven't yet)
- ▶ Unknown Knowns (knowledge that's available but unconsidered)
- ▶ Unknown Unknowns (often the deadliest of all, the things you "don't know that you don't know")

Starbucks' AI-driven Deep Brew platform illustrates the role that these four knowledge categories can play in business transformations.

- ▶ **Known Knowns.** Starbucks knows that digital engagement is a key strength; its loyalty app members contribute nearly half of its revenue. This knowledge led to a strategic conclusion: that data-driven personalization drives customer loyalty and growth.
- ▶ **Known Unknowns.** Thanks to Deep Brew's analytics, Starbucks recognized gaps in its capabilities, such as its ability to predict local demand shifts or fine-tune staffing store by store, and it actively invested in solutions.
- ▶ **Unknown Knowns.** Data analysis revealed that Starbucks held valuable information that it wasn't fully utilizing. For example, 43 percent of at-home tea drinkers add no sugar. This insight led to new unsweetened tea products.
- ▶ **Unknown Unknowns.** A completely unforeseen event— the Covid pandemic—caused customers to shift heavily to mobile orders and drive-throughs. Starbucks adapted by repurposing its datasets in real time, even tracking local vaccination rates to guide unexpected store format changes (like adding or subtracting drive-throughs and pickup-only locations). The organization's software-driven agility helped it navigate the disruption and seize emergent opportunities.

Bottom-up feedback loops are critical to ensuring that all four types of knowledge are in sync. Some of the worst intelligence failures (like September 11, 2001, in the US and October 7, 2023, in Israel) occur when the people on the ground suspect something is amiss but their reports don't reach decision-makers because of bureaucratic hurdles. Even more often, staff self-censor critical insights out of fear. AI's ability to share the right information with the right people at the right time makes a major difference.

Jonathan recalls an awkward occasion at HP when he recognized a potential market opportunity that senior decision-makers were ignoring.

It happened in 2009, when he sat down with an executive to discuss a critical touch screen component that was being developed by one of his clients. The reception he got was subdued. When Jonathan asked why HP wasn't pursuing the market for touch devices more aggressively, he was told that they were waiting for Apple to deploy the iPad so they could fast follow. And then, as Apple seized the future, HP waited for Microsoft to release an operating system that could compete with iOS. When that didn't work, it bought Palm, an also-ran, and tried to leverage its has-been operating system to compete in phones and tablets. When that failed, it tried releasing devices on Google's Android platform. A quarter or so later, those devices were on fire sale.

Today, Apple is worth 60 times HP and Hewlett Packard Enterprise combined. They could have dominated this market, yet they barely even played. HP rightly recognized that hardware is hard to develop organically and moves at the speed of global manufacturing supply chains. But it wrongly assumed it could use its heft to buy its way in.

HP lost because it did everything right. It carefully managed its risk profile, allowing other companies to make the expensive investments, while deploying its own capital only for knowable gains. But in failing to innovate and take risks, it lost the advantages that accrue to first movers. It saw the future, but it didn't understand its implications. AI certainly would have helped to develop that understanding in an unbiased way.[43]

SYNTAX VS. CONTEXT

HP, like most large enterprises, is highly reliant on standard operating procedures (SOPs). SOPs exist for a reason, which is to enable speed and scale; employees interfere with them at their peril. Like languages, those systems have two components—syntax and context. Syntax is typically rules-based, so people can understand it readily. But context is harder to parse and almost impossible to scale, as it depends on historical knowledge and local mores; unfortunately, it's also where some of the most important drivers and blockers of opportunities lie.

Stephen encountered this issue in 1999. The British company where he worked, Psion PLC, had invented the personal digital assistant or PDA back in the 1980s, and it was justifiably proud of its sophisticated technology. By 1999, Psion's PDAs could even send faxes (though why anyone would want to do that remains an open question). Stephen was tasked by the company's CEO, in quite clear syntax, to bring a smartphone to market quickly so that Psion could pioneer once again.

What was less clear was the context. Psion's customers had always been deep-pocketed; placing their Psion PDAs in front of them at a meeting signified real status. Given that context, the goal was to create a device that was even more high-end. It would have a color screen! And fast data connectivity! And games! As features were added, dependencies on outside suppliers grew and grew. Ultimately, a key software supplier let the company down, and the project was shelved prior to full production.

One lonely industrial designer had argued for a different course. Let's build a cheap device, he said, that can only make calls and send text messages and emails. Make it simple. Target teens and young adults, who were already starting to communicate that way, albeit with their clunky phones.

As visionary as he was (he was describing what the BlackBerry would soon become), the product the designer envisioned clashed with the company's context. "Good enough" didn't fit Psion's branding, customer relationships, sophisticated tech capabilities, or even its sales channels. He was ignored. Never mind that he was right.

AI can help prevent these kinds of mistakes in several ways:

1. **Translating context across boundaries.** By monitoring communications across functional silos and geographies, AI delivers unprecedented situational awareness, transforming obscure local context into actionable intelligence.
2. **Enabling intelligent rule-breaking.** AI provides a safety net when conditions seem to warrant a suspension of long-standing operating procedures, by calculating the risks and benefits of deviation.
3. **Accelerating collective intelligence.** AI connects previously isolated insights, experiments, and learnings throughout your organization. Think of it as a knowledge common, in which innovations from one "arm" of your organization can immediately benefit the others. And it can be trained to ask the tough questions that context often shunts aside.

The keys to unleashing these capabilities?

▸ Remove permission barriers between AI systems, so they can better talk to each other and bring more knowledge to bear.
▸ Democratize access to information across the enterprise, so more people have the benefit of it.
▸ Incentivize teams to share intelligence instead of hoarding it.

DESIGNING YOUR RNA TO INCREASE YOUR ADAPTABILITY

The ammonite couldn't change its shell. But an octopus is a shape-shifter; it can alter its color and form to mimic a flounder, a rock, or a piece of seaweed to fool predators and prey. Agile operations allow Octopus Organizations to shapeshift as well.

Because AI can handle complexity at scale, it can read and sort customer data in ways that allow for much more customization than human beings alone could manage. This enables, for instance, bespoke product selection and pricing. In highly competitive industries, continuous differentiation retains loyal customers and recruits new ones. As one example, the fast fashion giant Zara configures its supply chains and assembly lines for rapid retooling so it can bring out new products in weeks rather than months.

AI also helps humans capture the upside of uncertainty by evaluating the suitability of investment in products and capabilities. Deepinvent, for example, helps inventors analyze the intellectual property landscape for market opportunities.

AI can create sophisticated models to test assumptions, analyze, and advise. But human beings will still need to ask it the right questions. The most innovative companies follow a five-step process when experimenting:

1. First establish what you know, what you don't know and can't know (those known knowns and unknown unknowns), including any X factors that could disrupt everything (like a global pandemic).
2. Then, tease out the key hypotheses you want to test, making sure you're rooted in the Jobs to be Done of key customers and stakeholders.
3. Consider how the hypotheses can be tested (computer models; limited pilots with A/B panels; qualitative tests with in-depth interviews; etc.) and the metrics you will use to weigh the results. Ideally, you should design multiple testing processes targeted at distinct contexts, introducing a level of complexity that you would want to avoid if humans rather than AI had to analyze the results.
4. Weigh the potential costs and risks as well as the potential returns. Prioritize your initiatives accordingly.
5. Finally, set up a system that allows you to manage your innovation portfolio continuously, rapidly iterating or ending

initiatives based on your learnings. Remember, about 80 percent of venture capital investments have negative returns. Every experiment should have a reasonable chance of success, but if it's doomed to fail, let it fail sooner rather than later.

As we've established in earlier chapters, if you're in an AI-enabled Octopus Organization, both intelligence and initiative will be widely dispersed. You needn't be a senior manager to turn intelligence into adaptation and resilience, or even to introduce a modest new initiative.

Of course, organizations don't run on intelligence alone. Emotions are critical wherever humans collaborate. The next chapter focuses on that critical element.

Afførd Democratizes Customer Insights

Afførd used to march to the cadence of annual planning cycles. Stable product lines, big factories, and a network of stores meant that shifts could occur only gradually.

In the AI Age, customers expect far more flexibility in what they purchase and how they do it. The luxury of gradual change no longer exists. The pace of competitive innovation is continuous.

Recognizing this, Afførd focuses significant technology spend on getting closer to its customers so it can sense demand signals quickly. Its marketing team uses trend-sensing tools to trawl millions of interactions with its customers. AI agents have in-depth conversations with customers about product features. Afførd's online storefront also collects customer information. The firm's research team utilizes AI to synthesize historical PowerPoint decks (which are rarely used today), AI-developed reports, and real-time datasets into a searchable customer knowledge platform accessible to all Afførd employees.

The world has also become more unstable, a trend that began long before AI hit like a rogue wave. Fortunately, the company has a robust system for seeing what's next. Its ability to adapt in the face of changing demand and shifting supply chains has become a core competitive advantage.

CHAPTER SUMMARY

The pace of change is accelerating. To stay ahead, organizations must build capabilities in two areas:

- Sensing the external environment
- Maintaining a deep understanding of customer needs

AI can help your organization gather signals from within and without, mapping them in more detail than ever before. People need training to use these insights well. A more customer-centric approach to innovation is also needed. By blending AI's analytic power with the insights that arise from customer intimacy and agile experimentation, organizations can remain resilient and adaptable, even as the sea shifts beneath them.

SETTING THE RIGHT CULTURE

CHAPTER 6

An Emotional Being

Embrace disruption by building trust

Athena's suction is gentle, though insistent. It pulls me like an alien's kiss. Her melon-size head bobs to the surface and her left eye—octopuses have a dominant eye, as people have dominant hands—swivels in its socket to meet mine. Her black pupil is a fat hyphen in a pearly globe. Its expression reminds me of the look in the eyes of paintings of Hindu gods and goddesses: serene, all-knowing, heavy with wisdom stretching back before time. . . . Athena's is an exceptionally intimate embrace. She is at once touching and tasting my skin, and possibly the muscle, bone, and blood beneath. Though we have only just met, Athena already knows me in a way no being has known me before.

**—SY MONTGOMERY,
THE SOUL OF AN OCTOPUS[44]**

As alien as their makeup may seem to us, octopuses have emotions. They have distinct personalities and display consistent behaviors such as playfulness, aggression, curiosity, and affection. Their emotions seem to be shaped by their past experiences: For instance, they tend to display fear when revisiting locations where they were attacked.

The scientific evidence for these claims is quite strong.[45] And just as they do for humans, emotions seem to serve an evolutionary purpose for octopuses. They matter for their survival.

All that said, we humans can do something that octopuses can't. We work together, partly through engaging collective emotions, to create organizations that serve long-term goals. Whether those organizations are engaged in business, politics, academics, warfare, the arts, or religion, they are bigger, smarter, stronger, and more capable and powerful than the sum of their many parts.

The human ability to collaborate creates enormous advantages, but it also leads to emotionally-driven organizational dynamics that are resistant to change. Harvard Business School's John Kotter has argued that 70 percent of organizational transformation efforts fail.[46] That's because organizations, like the people who work in them, tend to get stuck in their ways.

Organizations don't resist change because the people who run them are bad at their jobs, as HBS Professor (and Stephen's mentor) Clayton Christensen famously observed, but because they tend to be so good at them. Many served their best customers so well and so successfully that they forgot about all the people they weren't serving, creating an opening for disruption.[47] Ask HP and Psion about that.

The transformations that Kotter and Christensen wrote about were often much less fundamental than what AI demands. In addition, AI provokes strong emotions in and of itself. Many employees understandably see it in much the same light that the nineteenth-century English weavers known as the Luddites saw steam-powered looms: as an existential threat to their livelihoods and, even more-so, to their human dignity. Like the displaced French workers who threw their wooden shoes or *sabots* into mills to disrupt production, the Luddites also committed sabotage. For many of us, our fear of nonhuman intelligence is seemingly as instinctive as our fear of snakes, as a host of archetypal narratives from *Frankenstein* to *The Terminator* illustrate.

But as challenging and emotionally wrenching as transformations are, the roughly 30 percent that succeed provide important lessons. Microsoft, for one, has reengineered both its product focus and its entire culture from top to bottom. Much of the credit goes to Satya Nadella. When he became its CEO in 2014, Nadella recognized the need to change, took ownership of it, and relentlessly and persuasively communicated it to employees and stakeholders.

Deep transformations can't be delegated to HR or pushed down to line managers because managers, as Kotter wrote, are trained and incentivized "to minimize risk and keep the current system operating," while change, "by definition, requires creating a new system."[48]

Corporate transformations can cost a lot and take time to show positive returns—as many as five to six years for large firms. That is longer than many CEOs stay in the job. And senior leaders are no more immune to emotions than the Luddites were. They have worked hard to reach the top. They too can feel threatened by AI and the move to a decentralized model. Few want to cede their authority to their newly empowered subordinates, and certainly not to machines.

Leaders must be credible, which means they must acknowledge that AI *will* in fact render some employees and their functions obsolete. They should provide generous support for the dislocated, not only because it's the right thing to do, but because those employees will still have important roles to play while the transition is underway.

Take IBM's approach to workforce reduction following an automation drive in 2023. That year, IBM announced that it would pause hiring for back-office roles. It estimated that 30 percent of certain jobs (roughly 7,800 positions) would be impacted by automation.[49]

The company offered career transition services such as resume building, interview coaching, and job matching in addition to severance packages. For employees who wanted to pivot into new roles, IBM offered training programs in data science, cloud computing, and cybersecurity—skills that would help the company deliver AI-driven services. Offering upskilling opportunities for new, high-demand roles is a powerful way to show that your organization is serious about retaining the skills, institutional memories, and wisdom of longtime employees.

While IBM's efforts were admirable, expecting accounting staff, say, to pivot to cloud computing or coding may have seemed like a bridge too far. But many staff can transition to adjacent roles. Look at people's skills and experience—rather than their job descriptions. Given that nearly a quarter of high performing staff are overlooked by traditional management reviews, there is surely low-hanging fruit.[50]

Up until now, it has been impractical to interview each impacted employee about their transferable skills, but AI can help tease out and frame up new opportunities in collaboration with them on a cost-effective basis.

THE RULES OF CULTURE

The written and unwritten rules that define and govern organizational cultures are infused with strong emotions. Acknowledge these rules and use them to foster change. As your first step, make a list of these rules. All of them had a purpose at one time; many no longer do. Once you make them explicit, those that no longer fit will be obvious.

Then consider: What new rules will you need to make your AI-infused Octopus Organization a reality? Few traditional companies offer clear templates. But many of the blockchain startups that are run as decentralized autonomous organizations (DAOs) do.

In a DAO, top-down control fades. Instead, small "tribes" follow rules that are baked into the organizational software. Code replaces thick agreements and sets the rules for joining, voting, and profit sharing (which is often disbursed in cryptocurrency). Teams are self-managing. Some DAOs struggle to scale; many—like most startups—are doomed to fail. Still, the tribe model is not that different from the way many consulting and law firms have been successfully organized for decades.[51]

Organizations that rely on AI for their operations also provide models. Look at high-frequency trading (HFT) firms. These firms rely on data analysis and market intelligence to identify arbitrage opportunities and capitalize on short-term price movements. Advanced computer programs execute thousands of trades, often within milliseconds or microseconds. HFT companies invest heavily in high-speed data feeds and low-latency network infrastructure to ensure that their orders reach exchanges in time. Risk management is crucial. Outcomes are continuously monitored so they can adjust risk parameters as needed and set limits on their trades to prevent excessive losses. They have rules, and humans play very essential roles, but the system has been designed for an AI-first environment.

CHANGING THE RULES

To set your own rules, get a read on what your employees think and feel about your current culture and its capacity to adapt to the proposed changes. Survey them. Ask them to respond to granular statements like these:

- ▶ "My organization has the flexibility to rapidly adjust when projects don't go as planned."
- ▶ "Our leaders model the right innovation behaviors and attitudes for others to follow."
- ▶ "I am concerned that AI will limit my influence at work."
- ▶ "I trust leadership to embrace AI in ways that will benefit me."

Share the results, respond to them honestly, and use those insights as you build your case for the changes. As you do, always frame the transition as an opportunity rather than a threat.

Then train selected groups of senior, middle, and "edge" customer-facing managers on the changes you need to institute, so they can evangelize, role model, and train others in turn. These champions should be drawn not just from IT, but from every function that will use AI and whose jobs will change because of it. Give them a pilot initiative to carry out, preferably one that can deliver an early confidence-building win that can be celebrated widely. But make sure it's targeted narrowly, so that an early failure can be contained and turned into a learning experience. Track the emotions of your stakeholders' employees, customers, and suppliers alike—and respond to them appropriately.

Remember, culture change is like a brick wall. The bricks are all the things that managers can measure and control via clear decisions. Culture is the less tangible mortar that holds the bricks together. It governs the innumerable behaviors and thought processes that get people aligned around what to do next.

To change your culture, you can't just talk about building the wall. You must actually change the way of working—the bricks and the mortar are both essential. Without changing the more tangible and visible factors, softer behaviors and ways of thinking simply won't transform. Culture exists for a reason, so you need to change the reasons why the culture is the way it is. Mortar without bricks creates a puddle, not a wall.

The Ingredients of Culture Change

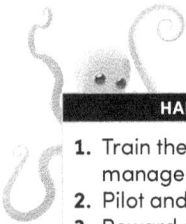

HARD LEVERS (BRICKS)	SOFT LEVERS (MORTAR)
1. Train the edge, middle, and senior management 2. Pilot and role model 3. Reward smart experimentation and measure learnings achieved 4. Promote the internal entrepreneurs 5. Provide resources for entrepreneurial initiatives	1. Deal with the inevitable setbacks as learning experiences to be embraced, not as times to scapegoat 2. Frame the transition as opportunity, not threat (There will likely be more wealth creation in the AI Age than at any previous time in human history.) 3. Model the behaviors you want to see, including using the technology 4. Create a community of like-minded innovators

CASE STUDY: Princess Cruises Tackles Technology Culture Change

Well before AI became widespread, Princess Cruises used technology to eliminate one of its customers' biggest pain points—the amount of time they wasted waiting in lines. In doing so, they modeled an approach to developing, deploying, and scaling change.

Cruise ships have a lot in common with long-established organizations of scale. They are big and complicated and notoriously un-nimble. When under full steam, it takes five miles to bring one to a full stop, and ten miles to turn one around. To manage the complexity of their operations, each of their hundreds of crew and service providers must follow strict protocols.

Developing the technological fix for excessive lines was relatively easy and low-tech compared to AI. If every passenger carried a small electronic token that could be identified and tracked by the crew, then they could be counted automatically as they moved about the ship. Waiters could greet them by name; housekeepers would know when their cabin was unoccupied and ready to clean. The passengers could use the tokens instead of keys to open the doors of their staterooms and instead of cash or their credit cards to pay for drinks and souvenirs.

It was a transformative innovation, but it was expensive and complicated. Deploying it on a single ship took four years, 75 miles of cable, 7,000 sensors, and a host of training sessions. So how did Princess Cruises develop this game-changing idea and then roll it out to all eighteen of its ships, with their 30,000 employees?

It did so by focusing simultaneously on two tasks: perfecting and building out the technology, and then transforming its internal culture so employees would become comfortable with this new way of doing things.

The innovation team in charge of designing and implementing it (whose leader reported directly to Princess Cruises'

C-Suite) started out by building a mock ship in a converted military facility in Florida. Then they recruited designers and programmers to develop the devices and pulled some of their most talented frontline staff—captains, entertainment directors, restaurant managers—off their ships so they could work alongside them. A hotel manager described the experience:

> On ships, we know what is going to happen on what date and when. . . . Everything works like clockwork. I could look up every rule and regulation and know what to expect. [Here] there were no regulations, an agile environment that was about failing fast and moving on. Some days we would have failures . . . then the next day we'd have a breakthrough . . . Guests have no idea of the blood, sweat, and tears that went into this.[52]

When it came time to roll the technology out across the entire fleet, the frontline staff that had been a part of the development process became ambassadors and trainers. Employees were far more open to learning from their peers than from strangers. "We humans don't like changes," one of the ship captains that participated in the process remarked.

> But once people see that the system is working properly and that there is benefit, then they support it. We rolled this out very slowly; we didn't just turn this on overnight. First, we installed the sensors that opened guest doors. We installed it in just one section on one deck of one ship. We piloted that, tested it, improved it. Only then did we expand it to other sections, then other decks. . . . Then we moved on. But the next application came much faster because everyone understood what was coming.[53]

Hardwiring a cruise ship to read passengers' tokens is a far more straightforward challenge than reorganizing the governance, work methods, and culture of an entire enterprise. And given the layoffs that may well be part of the AI transition, it will be much harder to sell.

But AI will come with an unexpected benefit. Octopus Organizations thrive on a culture of what we call "strategic serendipity"—a way of thinking and operating that reduces risk and improves the odds of success. If having more, bigger and better wins is not a positive way to frame the need to embrace AI, then we don't know what is.

Strategic serendipity comes with still another benefit that's even more surprising and that we will learn more about in the next chapter.

Afførd's Transformation Process

The change process hasn't been easy for Afførd, but it was much harder for many of its competitors.

Afførd's differentiator was the early work it did on cultural transformation. Its leadership team recognized that you can't rip-and-replace a culture. It took the time to think deeply about its implicit as well as its explicit rules and norms, and studied other legacy organizations that had come through similarly massive changes intact.

It was careful about choosing which aspects of the transformation to prioritize and which could be allowed to lag. Then, starting with its IT function, it proceeded deliberately, building momentum while maintaining its clarity of destination and purpose.

Before insisting on softer types of behavioral and mindset shifts, it focused on the hard levers of change:

- Rules
- Reporting relationships
- Capabilities
- Incentives

Change keeps getting faster. Company leaders see that nonstop change creates stress and uncertainty for employees. They listen to those worries and model the new habits required. As software takes over more routine tasks, its leaders' human strengths—empathy, judgment, and clear communication—are what set them apart.

Afford demonstrates that change is hard yet possible, given the right leadership.

CHAPTER SUMMARY

Embracing AI requires leaders to acknowledge emotional resistance, communicate transparently, and address the cultural norms that shape an organization, not just the operational systems. Successful transformations, as shown by companies like Microsoft and Princess Cruises, depend on credible leadership, grassroots involvement, and visible, iterative wins. Successful culture changes are framed as an opportunity, not a threat. Shifts in structure, roles, and incentives are necessary for culture change. Building a strong wall requires both "bricks" and "mortar."

CHAPTER 7

Strategic Serendipity

Increase success by leaning into uncertainty

*"The greatest danger in times of turbulence is not the
turbulence—it is to act with yesterday's logic."*

—PETER DRUCKER

Whether they are editing their RNA in real time or changing their shapes and colors, octopuses are optimized for resilience and adaptability. But octopuses owe their very existence to an improbable stroke of luck. Though some larger species produce just dozens of eggs, most produce hundreds of thousands. Many of those eggs never hatch, and only 1 percent of the hatchlings survive to adulthood.

Humans, thankfully, face better odds. One reason we thrive, as we've seen, is because we cooperate, combining and multiplying our individual efforts over space and time. Our species started collaborating in small teams. Then we organized by combining those teams. Alone, we build sandcastles. Together, we build cathedrals.

A second reason is our ability to enhance and even increase our supply of luck. How is that possible? *Webster's* defines luck as a product of chance, and chance as "something that happens unpredictably without discernible human intention or observable cause." Our answer is that luck isn't all chance and isn't quite magic. Nor must it be a product of celestial favor.

Luck is probabilistic—much like transformer models, the technology upon which generative AI rests. Nothing is ever assured. One outcome enables another set of possibilities stacked atop another, ad infinitum. Much as transformers can be improved by weighing the likelihood of critical outcomes, so can luck. In a casino, if you engineer luck by counting cards or loading dice, that's called cheating. In business, the entire game is to change the rules; that's called innovation. In tech, casinos, and business, the math is the same: you make small changes at the right places at the right time. Together, they radically shift the network's dynamics.

Inspired by a Persian folktale, "The Three Princes of Serendip," Horace Walpole coined the word *serendipity* in the eighteenth century to refer to the discovery "by accident and sagacity" of something someone was "not in quest of."

Serendip is the old Arabic name for the country now called Sri Lanka. In the story, its three princes journey from there to Persia, where they hear about a missing camel. When they find its trail, they deduce from a variety of physical clues that the camel was lame, blind in one eye, laden with honey and butter, and carrying a pregnant woman as its rider. When they share those insights with its owner, he accuses them of stealing it themselves, hauls them before the emperor, and demands that they be executed. As the princes explain how they came by their knowledge, a traveler walks in and announces that he has just found the missing beast. The emperor not only spares the princes, he rewards them with positions in his court. The traveler's entrance and the emperor's largesse were purely matters of chance, but the princes had laid the groundwork for both with their seeming prescience. As Louis Pasteur once put it, "chance favors only the prepared mind."

So how can you change your odds?

In a casino, the odds are stacked in the house's favor, but for some games, like blackjack, its advantage is relatively modest. It shrinks even more when a player is skilled, and if a skilled player counts cards, the odds flip the other way. The advantage that card counters have over the house is small (about 1 percent), but it can add up over enough well-played hands.

AI allows you to count your cards at an almost limitless scale by tracking trends and constantly weighing and reweighing probabilities. You might say, "That's not luck, that's science," but that is exactly our point. Tilt the odds the right way and do it consistently, and you can change your outcomes.

Strategic serendipity comes with another benefit, too, that may be even more surprising. While it's all about winning, it isn't inherently cynical or zero-sum; in fact, it is a driver of altruism. That's because it depends on collaboration and community building. As it turns out, building effective networks creates more and better possibilities for everyone.

In our analysis of 2.7 million leadership surveys, conducted with the Harrison Assessment team, we discovered a striking pattern: only one in seven managers consistently outperformed their peers during times of disruptive change. What made the difference wasn't their IQ or length of tenure; it was a distinct set of repeatable behaviors that helped them cut through ambiguity, capitalize on momentum, and guide their people forward. Those behaviors are the focus of this chapter.

Managers who disproportionately succeeded *leveraged help, used their connections, controlled chaos,* and *knew what was missing*— four habits and tools that helped them manage complexity, drive clarity amid confusion, and manufacture their own lucky breaks. Conveniently, these behaviors spell LUCK.

The LUCK Framework at a Glance

	CORE BEHAVIOR	KEY TAKEAWAY
Leverage Help	Ask for help from your peers.	Decentralized, psychologically safe teams pivot faster during crises because they create more options.
Use Your Connections	Build diverse socioeconomic and industry-spanning relationships.	The right network architectures accelerate innovation and recovery after shocks.
Control Chaos	Use a first principles approach to managing risk.	Standard operating procedures might be useless in a changed situation.
Know What's Missing	Ask counterfactual questions before taking action.	Systematic gapspotting reduces risk and surfaces white space opportunities.

THE FLAVORS OF SERENDIPITY

Luck comes in three flavors: the luck we are given, the luck we make, and the luck we give. There's nothing we can do about the first except to be certain that we take full advantage of whatever endowment of it we have. But there is a leprechaun's pot of tactics you can use to make your own luck—and even more importantly, to point you to the most beneficial risks to take.

An even more important driver of luck is what we give to each other. That's because abundance doesn't come from taking but from sharing. A large body of evidence suggests that humans are as wired for altruism as for competition.[54] So many of us don't avail ourselves of even a tenth of the bounty that our family, our friends, our colleagues, and even strangers are willing to give us; we remain focused on scarcity.

Luck is *not* a finite resource. We make it and then augment it through sharing it amongst ourselves. We do so through the following LUCK behaviors.

Leverage Help

Repeatedly successful people know the limits of their knowledge and skills. They fill the gaps by choosing the right mentors, collaborators, and advisors, whether human or machine.

While proprietary matters cannot be discussed with competitors, leaders of Octopus Organizations encourage all their employees to step outside of their functional silos and learn from each other. Then they take their own advice and venture out of their C-suites themselves to learn from their division and regional heads, domain experts, and their peers in other industries. They seek reverse mentoring from younger digital natives as well.

Stephen once worked with the head of a large credit card issuer. This executive viewed reams of evidence that his company would greatly boost its transaction volume if it reduced its merchant charges. Being a wise person, he feared that cutting them would be an irreversible mistake. So he got out of his office and asked for help. He walked down the main street of a tony Chicago suburb and asked twenty storeowners for advice. They didn't just complain about the fees—they offered real input, peer to peer. His confidence bolstered, the executive made the tough decision to reduce the charges, and billions of dollars of new revenues followed.

How can you give your people the freedom to ask for help? According to the sixth edition of *The Handbook of Social Psychology*:

- ▸ Psychological safety predicts team learning and error reporting.
- ▸ People who seek advice on hard problems are judged more competent, not less.

Harvard Business School's Amy Edmondson says the first step that leaders can take to convince their people to collaborate is "calling attention to the nature of the work"—emphasizing that silence is riskier than speaking up:

> You [must set] the stage to remind people [that] we're not in the industrial era anymore, where your job is to just keep

your head down and do it exactly as specified. Now we're in the knowledge era, the digital era, where your job is to team up with other people, to navigate uncertainty in an ongoing way. You simply can't do that work well unless you lower your guard and speak up."[55]

She urges leaders to model this behavior by asking "What concerns do you have?"—a question that presumes that everyone on the team has input. By making silence awkward, it encourages considered responses.

Adopting the following practices will help you to leverage help from your network:

PRACTICE TOOLS TO LEVERAGE HELP

1. **Asking as a public ritual.** Open meetings with questions like, "What am I missing?" and "Who can help?"
2. **Reverse mentoring.** Encourage younger digital natives to share their understandings with more senior managers. Exchanging AI fluency for contextual wisdom is a win-win proposition.
3. **Trusting, but verifying, your AI advisor.** Make sure you probe your AI agent with questions like "List pitfalls that experts overlook." Compare its answers with human answers in team meetings.

Use Your Connections

When your goal is to innovate or to solve for ambiguity, the best answer is rarely the most obvious one. So ask better questions of more people. If you're not sure where to go, ask your AI helper. Or look across your org chart and your broader network. Its size matters less than its diversity. A small, well-curated set of connections spanning industries, functions, and backgrounds radically increases your odds of catching a signal that others miss. Frame your questions carefully. They will lead you to more interesting places than you can imagine alone.

Consider the Swiss engineer George de Mestral. One day in 1948, he returned from a walk in the woods covered in burrs. Most of us would have simply pulled them off. De Mestral examined the burrs under a microscope instead and saw the hook and loop pattern that made them stick. It took him a decade and the help of a professional weaver to turn that observation into the fastening fabric that we now know as Velcro.

In complex environments, luck favors the curious—especially if they are well networked. You don't have to be close to someone to benefit from your contact with them. Mark Granovetter's classic research on "the strength of weak ties" shows that news about job opportunities is more likely to travel via acquaintances, not best friends.[56] Dormant tie studies extend this: Reactivating old contacts yields more actionable advice than polling current colleagues.

When networking speak less, listen more. As IE University's Santiago Iñiguez cautions, "If you are a very charismatic leader, you may dominate the conversation. . . . You have to draw in the introverts, because they have some of the best ideas." Inclusive questioning brings out insights that might otherwise stay buried.

PRACTICE TOOLS FOR USING CONNECTIONS

- ▶ **30-day Dormant Tie Pings.** Reach out to at least one lapsed contact every month.
- ▶ **Network Map Audit.** Ask your AI assistant to color-code your contacts by their functions and industries. Ask it to identify first-order connections on LinkedIn who have friends in areas that you're weak in and set up coffees with them.
- ▶ **Connection Brokering.** Set a KPI for yourself: Arrange introductions between two unconnected peers every month.
- ▶ **LinkedIn Roulette.** Every week, set up a twenty-minute conversation with an interesting person whom you do not know.

Control Chaos

The fossil record is filled with examples of shocks that caused species like the ammonite to fail; so are the annals of business. Disruption is all about the ability to manage change.

A big part of strategic luck is sensing when you need to change yourself, your environment, your networks, and your plans so that you can take advantage of the upside and manage the downside of whatever happens.

Always look for the opportunities that can be hidden in crises. Harvard Business School Professor Clark Gilbert did extensive research into why certain newspapers thrived with the advent of the internet, even while most struggled or closed.[57] He found that the deciding factor wasn't their balance sheets but their mindsets. Newspapers with leaders who viewed digital as a threat defended their legacy businesses and fell behind. Those who viewed it as an opportunity to expand restructured early and captured new markets.

The same logic applies to you and your team. If you treat every surprise as a threat, you'll be paralyzed. If you treat it as a potential fulcrum for change, then you are more likely to capture opportunities.

Roger Martin, the former dean of the Rotman School of Business at the University of Toronto, once worked with a mining company. Its leaders had gotten bogged down in a heated debate.[58] One contingent wanted to shut down a mine; the other to expand it. Martin reframed the discussion. Instead of arguing about who's right, he asked, "What would have to be true for each option to make sense?" That simple shift turned a fight over binaries into a shared investigation. What they uncovered broke the deadlock.

PRACTICE TOOLS FOR CONTROLLING CHAOS

▶ **Chaos Compass.** How do you navigate a volatile, uncertain, complex, and ambiguous (VUCA) world? By countering volatility with vision, uncertainty with understanding, complexity with clarity, and ambiguity with agility.

▶ **Red Team Drills.** Stress-test your plan by assigning a small group to model it and see what would break it before reality does the same.

▶ **Daily Pulse.** Every day, devote 15 minutes with your team to sharing new data or different perspectives, adjusting your micro-priorities and broadening your thinking.

Know What's Missing

Perhaps the biggest part of luck is knowing how to recognize and seize opportunities that others miss. To do this, you need to recognize the gaps that need to be filled, which is where uncontested opportunities lie.

Doing this requires you to look beyond data (which is largely about the world as it exists today) and find the white spaces. Stephen remembers a mistake from early in his consulting career, when he researched the market for flat-screen TVs in the mid-1990s. Industry sales were miniscule. When surveyed, consumers expressed zero interest in buying a temperamental product that would cost $5,000 and, weirdly, be hung on a wall like a painting. Instead of looking at the market for flat-screen TVs at that nascent stage—when they were overpriced and delivered so-so performance—he should have looked ahead to what they *could* be and how they could satisfy consumers' unrecognized Jobs to be Done, like impressing the neighbors.

Jonathan has found that two questions consistently help him and his clients think differently:

▶ How would my opinion change if some of my facts turned out to be untrue?

▶ How would my actions change if something new came to light?

In an interview, Ward Cunningham, who invented the Wiki, suggested a third question:

> ▸ What would happen if I started at the end or middle instead of the beginning?

Changing where one starts thinking through a challenge often leads to a new perspective.

It's important to police for bias, because the latest research in organizational psychology tells us that leaders skew toward false negatives on novel ideas, dismissing as impossible many innovations that could in fact succeed. Humans are nearly incapable of eliminating their own bias without external input. Historically, the surest protection against bias was peer review. That still works, but your AI can accomplish the same thing faster—if you ask it to.

PRACTICE TOOLS TO KNOW WHAT'S MISSING

> ▸ **Premortem Worksheet.** Imagine what failure would look like. Try to find three overlooked factors and address them.
> ▸ **First Principles Canvas.** Break your problem into its basic components and look for opportunities to solve each one individually.
> ▸ **Abductive Duo Questions.** Abductive reasoning is when you attempt to derive a probable conclusion from something that can be observed. Ask yourself and your team: If our core assumption is false, what changes? What new signal would force us to pivot?

PUTTING LUCK INTO PRACTICE

AI-driven analytics can reveal blind spots, but it's culture that determines whether we do something about them. Cultures that reward curiosity (rather than just execution) and ask what might have been missed are the ones best suited to evolve and grow.

Developing the four levers of LUCK and integrating them with emotional intelligence, trust, and AI-enabled insights will allow your organization to act less like Einstein's definition of insanity—doing the same thing over and over again while expecting different results—and more like an octopus: a living, feeling creature that continually adapts.

All of this matters greatly, because our civilization needs more luck, just as it needs AI. Over the past century, much of the world has enjoyed improvements in longevity, health, and income that our great-grandparents could not have imagined. But they have come at a steep cost to our planet, which is not just facing an environmental reckoning, but economic and political challenges. With a billion more people around the world poised to join the middle class, the increase in extractive resource use could be cataclysmic. The US government anticipates that the country will need to triple its nuclear power capacity by 2050 to support AI and data center growth,[59] while using *fewer* resources.

The path forward won't come from either a lone genius or a process-driven bureaucracy, but from the shared insights of networks of people collaborating with AI systems. Building denser networks of ideas and talent and tying them together with AI makes serendipity both more likely and more useful.

That's the job now: to design organizations—and societies—that get luckier on purpose. Because luck isn't a roll of the dice. It's a discipline and a choice, and the stakes have never been higher.

CHAPTER SUMMARY

While luck may seem random, organizations can actively improve their luck through intentional behaviors: what we call *strategic serendipity*. AI helps tilt the odds further by surfacing patterns, testing assumptions, and uncovering white spaces, but success also depends on human habits: Leveraging help, Using connections to build diverse networks, Controlling chaos by finding the opportunities hidden in disruptions, and Knowing what's missing—the LUCK framework.

The most impactful form of luck at an organizational level is shared abundance, the notion that we increase one another's odds of finding success through collaboration and sharing. By baking LUCK into your processes, your organization can turn unpredictability into a competitive edge. It won't just survive disruption; it will thrive on it.

BEGINNING YOUR JOURNEY

CHAPTER 8

Your Transformation Plan

*Lead your AI transformation with
a step-by-step roadmap*

*Although 80 percent of businesses view AI as a "core"
technology,[60] only 15 percent of employees believe that
their leaders have a clear strategy for its adoption.[61]*

"AI is probably the most important thing humanity has ever worked on," says Google CEO Sundar Pichai. "I think of it as more profound than electricity or fire."[62]

We agree, with one caveat. Companies that expect AI alone to drive transformation will be sorely disappointed. Adding AI to old systems may lift efficiencies, but that unlocks only a fraction of the technology's power.

Making the most of any new technology requires holistic, systemic changes in how that technology is used. Think of electricity. A century and a half ago, you couldn't just "plug in" electric lights. First, a deep-pocketed innovator like Thomas Edison had to erect a power plant and run cables down your street. Next, your house needed wiring, circuit breakers, switches, outlets, and sockets. Finally, your family had to quit using candles and whale-oil lamps and learn not to touch bare wires or spill water on them.

Factory owners ripped out steam engines and replaced them with electric motors. They retrained workers to run the new equipment, and, because the new machines could do so much more, reinvented many of their other processes. Some jobs vanished, and new roles appeared. As electricity spread, customers demanded electric products and services. The competitive landscape didn't just accelerate, it was completely reinvented. Many companies became unrecognizable as their former selves.

AI (and each breakthrough that follows) demands the same full-scale shift, but over years rather than decades. Think back to the shelled ammonite and the flexible octopus. Ammonites clung to hard armor, while octopuses shed their shells and wired intelligence through all eight of their arms—and sixty-six million years later, they're still going strong.

AI-ready companies mirror the octopus's design. The early movers may look strange, even alien, but they prove their mettle. Digital natives like Google, Meta, and Amazon were born amidst such an evolutionary explosion. None have completed the transformation, but they point the way. Older firms still carry ammonite habits. The species that follow must crack the shell, grow agile arms, and wire in shared intelligence. Then they will show what AI-plus-human networks can deliver.

History can be a guide here too. There's a saying: Businesses should avoid being the proverbial "buggy whip maker" in a world of automobiles.[63] Indeed, most buggy whip makers went out of business when cars replaced horses. But there was one, in France, that rode the wave of change successfully. Emile-Maurice, the head of his family-owned firm, declared to his team, "We are not a museum." He got out of his office and leveraged help from outside, even traveling to Detroit to meet with Henry Ford.

Then he invested in new ventures, such as using the company's sophisticated leather-making capabilities to make large bags that people could carry in those new cars they were buying. He knew his customers tastes very well and found ways to use the skills that his workforce had built up over decades to cater to new needs.

He also sought new capabilities that he felt customers would value. For instance, he hired silk weavers who designed scarves for the drivers of open-topped cars. He invented the windbreaker and transformed both luggage and clothing manufacturing through investments in new technologies like the zipper. You may not have known his story, but you know his company. It's still family-controlled, and today it's worth over $200 billion. Emile-Maurice's last name was Hermès. Like Emile-Maurice, you too will need to execute your transformation in steps.

Where should your transformation journey begin? While the path toward an Octopus Organization will look different for each company, we recommend five basic phases. Those phases are largely sequential, although there may be some overlap among them, particularly if different parts of the business have already taken some steps forward.

PHASE ONE: DEFINE THE VISION

The process begins with a clear-eyed look at the ways AI will alter your growth strategy. This first phase includes the following steps.

1. Understand Your Strategy in the Context of AI

As a leadership team, ask the challenging questions up front. This is the time to assess the full landscape.

- How will AI transform your customers' needs and the market's competitive dynamics?
- Where can AI boost your current edge? How could it fix past weak spots?
- As you grow more nimble, what new performance vectors should you pursue?
- Should your core customers or key capabilities shift?
- Which adjacent markets should you enter?

Assess each question both for your competitive environment five years from now, then for next year.

If these questions look similar to those you may have already posed when building your strategy, that's the point. An AI approach that sits outside of your core strategy will be suboptimal. Frame these questions around the technology, but don't box yourself in. As we've emphasized throughout this book, it must be embraced within the larger context of your organization.

2. Define and Weigh Your Choices

Since strategy is fundamentally about choice, distill the new strategic picture into a set of clear alternatives. The time to evaluate your options around potential new business models is today, as big bets involving growth and resilience take time to mature and pay off. Your AI adoption plans needn't involve a complete rethink of your growth strategy from day one. But as our friends at Afførd discovered back in Chapter 1, you do need to know which way you are heading. Do not assume it's the same as it was before AI became a part of the picture.

3. Open up the Process and Make Decisions

Next, invite representatives from across your organization to planning meetings. Ask these people to surface blind spots that you and other leaders may have missed, and listen to what frontline teams are saying about the potential pros and cons of AI adoption. Be transparent about the need to gather data and reward constructive dissent. Build a culture in which people share ownership of the transformation.

Then make decisions about where you'll head and what you'll prioritize—preferably in confidential group discussions rather than publicly, because some of the choices may be hard and controversial.

4. Assess Organizational Readiness

Focusing on parts of the business that are a high priority for AI integration and transformation, chart existing decision-making processes and workflows. Look at what teams actually do, not what their playbooks claim (because let's be honest, how many salespeople are following their playbooks letter by letter?). List major workflows, the tools in use, and key skills that each step demands.

Then, home in on where in this map AI can automate or boost results. Consider light-touch options like chatbots as well as more involved systems such as AI-driven knowledge management. Finally, ensure that the technology you review supports your stated AI vision. (For guidance on how to scale AI initiatives in a repeatable way, such as through a common technology stack, see the Appendix.)

5. Estimate Investments

Tally the costs and estimate the timelines for adoption, wrapping in the training, reskilling, and hiring needs already articulated. In most cases, the workload will be especially heavy for your HR and Learning and Development (L&D) teams—what support and resources do they require?

6. Identify Success Metrics

At the end of this journey, what will success mean, and how will you measure it? If you don't know the true stakes of change and can't track your progress toward it, you are unlikely to achieve real reinvention.

- Set financial targets and clear metrics in parallel.
- Define what success looks like at the journey's end.
- Decide how you will track it over time.
- Measure shorter cycle times and new AI-driven revenue.
- Track employee sentiment through surveys.
- Monitor your brand's value to your customers.

7. Create a Timeline for your AI Vision

Once you see where AI fits into your overall strategy, map a timeline for change. Ground it in your capabilities and your industry's realities. Heavily regulated sectors may move slowly, while digital natives may already be sprinting ahead.

Speak to a diverse range of external experts who are hands-on with AI technology and related organizational change. Choose realistic milestones, and be specific—what must your organization accomplish this quarter, this year, and in three or five years? Expect some efforts to fail and leave time to learn and adjust.

8. Share the Vision

Once your AI goals and timeline are clear, share the vision across the company. Stress the urgency, promise, and seriousness of the change. Go beyond slides and spreadsheets and have real two-way conversations with managers, team leads, and engineers beyond the C-suite.

Consider the softer side of communications. For instance, tie the AI story to the firm's purpose and values. Name worries without letting them dominate. Help people discover how your bold ideas still honor core principles.

Developing a shared language helps people grasp priorities, spot conflicts, and know when to escalate. If you lack a formal values statement, you might borrow from Amazon's Leadership Principles. Of these, "Invent and Simplify," "Are Right, A Lot," and "Learn and Be Curious" are perhaps the most important.

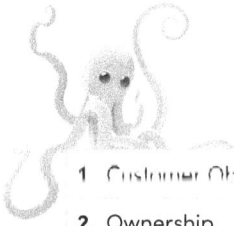

Amazon's
16 Leadership Principles

1. Customer Obsession
2. Ownership
3. Invent and Simplify
4. Are Right, A Lot
5. Learn and Be Curious
6. Hire and Develop the Best
7. Insist on High Standards
8. Think Big

9. Bias for Action
10. Frugality
11. Earn Trust
12. Dive Deep
13. Have Backbone and Commit
14. Deliver Results
15. Be Earth's Best Employer
16. Be Socially Responsible

PHASE TWO: PREPARE THE ORGANIZATION FOR CHANGE

Once it is clear what your organization intends to use AI to achieve over time, get tactical about where it adds real value. Identify what you need to do to embed it effectively.

1. Build Your Talent Plan

Take stock of the skills gaps that AI adoption will create. Map out skills by role and seniority in as much detail as you can. Senior leaders should not be exempt from this exercise.

> ▸ What skills will AI make redundant?
> ▸ How many people will need to be upskilled or reskilled, and in what ways?
> ▸ Can these employees shift to other types of work within your organization?
> ▸ What does AI adoption require from employees?
> ▸ Which middle managers will need to shift into coaching and manager-contributor roles?

While there will almost certainly be headcount reductions in some areas, you may experience an overall net gain of workers. As Travelers Chief Technology and Operations Officer Mojgan Lefebvre put it to us, "Most new technologies haven't necessarily resulted in the number of humans needed in general to do work becoming less. It's been more. You may eliminate some forms of work, but now there's a need for people to do other things."

Offer AI literacy training to both technical and nontechnical teams. AI touches a huge range of functions and moves quickly. A shared learning journey will smooth collaboration across the organization. Workers who know how to create new value will view AI as an asset, not a threat.

2. Find Your AI Champions

Pick or hire people who will drive AI adoption, governance, and change in the following areas:

- ▶ Senior leaders to own the vision
- ▶ Middle managers to execute and ensure appropriate AI adoption within their teams (See Chapter 2)
- ▶ Specialists to map details and keep projects moving—being careful, however, to keep AI adoption homegrown and not imposed by an army of transient outsiders

Build an "AI ambassador" network across departments. These are employees from different departments who are early adopters and can train and advocate to their peers. For example, a large bank introduced AI-based process automation and appointed champions in each operations team to learn the tool first, build a simple bot, and then encourage colleagues by demonstrating the time saved on mundane tasks. Peer learning can greatly accelerate AI adoption and help ensure that its tools are used responsibly.

3. Agree on Initial AI Experimentation

Identify parts of the organization that should serve as test beds for AI experiments—higher impact, lower risk implementations. You've likely undertaken some of this already, but as you scale up you can make these decisions on a larger canvas. As we emphasize in Phase Three, avoid "Pilot Hell" in which you have hundreds of disconnected initiatives with little guiding strategy, shared learning, or logic around when to grow or terminate your projects. This is a call for disciplined experimentation, not random pilots.

Ask yourself:

▶ Should you assemble a cross-functional design and engineering team?

▶ How will your AI-enabled teams interact?

▶ What changes must be made in your systems to ensure that a successful initiative can be scaled across the enterprise?

Recent work by the Stanford University Social and Language Technologies Lab suggests that workers "generally prefer high levels of human agency" in the tasks they most prefer to use AI to accomplish.[64] Perhaps start there, assessing a tool that augments rather than automates an existing workflow.

Overall, this step should be clarified by the work you have done in Phase One. With a clear sense of how AI weaves into your strategy, you have a focus. Ideally, you will be able to judge potential experiments based on whether they actually help drive that strategy, or serve as a distraction.

PHASE THREE: DESIGN AND LAUNCH AN EXPERIMENTATION PROGRAM

Your firm may have tried AI pilots already. That is not the same as having a standing, disciplined experimentation and learning program. A well-designed program keeps small, low-cost trials running so it can probe key unknowns and learn quickly. It helps the company keep pace in a field that changes daily.

Once you select the teams and use cases for experiments, make some clear decisions.

- ▶ What is the minimum you need to do to attain the learnings? Your goal is to learn prior to investing in making things perfect.
- ▶ How long will each test run, given an overall five-year AI horizon?
- ▶ How will you decide if it worked—and what happens if it flops?
- ▶ What technologies will drive toward your organization's AI vision?

Choose measures that match your AI vision, not just efficiency gains. Possible metrics include the following:

- ▶ **Efficiency gains:** time saved per task, case closure rates, or reduction in backlog
- ▶ **Accuracy and quality gains:** error rate reductions, false positive/negative rates
- ▶ **Compliance and risk outcomes:** quality metrics, fewer or less severe audit issues, regulatory compliance
- ▶ **Adoption and usage metrics:** AI utilization rates, number of times an AI recommendation was overridden by a human
- ▶ **Management and training metrics:** fewer escalations, faster ramp-up time for new team members, qualitative assessments of work quality
- ▶ **Workforce impacts:** Net Promoter Scores, work satisfaction, qualitative feedback on usefulness and trust
- ▶ **Skills gaps:** lack of understanding of how to use AI effectively, or to coach teams on proper AI usage

Technical metrics matter, but they are not enough. Judge early AI tests by core KPIs. Your goal is bigger than incremental gains or quick wins. You're building knowledge and skills for large-scale change. Use your success criteria to set your scaling speed. If a tool cuts overhead 5 percent instead of 20, adjust the next step.

Keep running experiments, even as your full-scale deployments grow. Each new AI wave brings fresh lessons, and you should learn in real time.

PHASE FOUR: BUILD SUPPORT INFRASTRUCTURE

While experiments run, ready the company to embed AI across teams and decisions. This means building or refining needed support:

- ▶ Data sharing infrastructure, storage systems, networking, and potentially machine learning (ML) platforms and Machine Learning Operations (MLOps) tools
- ▶ An organization-wide AI governance framework, setting guardrails and best practices on what information your models can access, who has access to what information, and what decisions should and should not be made using AI (as with data sharing infrastructure, this step can also come earlier if you are ready for it)
- ▶ Learning and Development resources identified in Step Two (Assess Organizational Readiness)
- ▶ A senior coalition to own and drive AI adoption

PHASE FIVE: OVERSEE CHANGE MANAGEMENT

As your AI journey matures, move your workforce toward decentralized adaptive work. You should have been working to reshape your culture from early on, but you'll need to accelerate your efforts as the tech foundation solidifies. This process includes the following steps.

1. Establish Your Leadership Style

Leaders keep a distributed organization healthy by signaling who owns what. Recall the Analytic, Agile, and Aligned Hearts. Know which heart to use in each context. Use Agile and Alignment approaches instead of Analytic processes whenever possible.

The C-suite should own mainly high-level or privileged matters such as union negotiations or acquisitions. Be very specific about the limits of executive control to prevent a gradual reversion to default behaviors.

As AI moves beyond pilots, set your own to-dos in the following areas:

- ▶ List the big AI opportunities and threats you face.
- ▶ Track early signals as they emerge.
- ▶ Plan how to seize opportunities and blunt risks.
- ▶ Adjust your role as needed.

Keep a list of key topics and review it often.

2. Encourage Iteration

Track key success metrics closely and encourage frank cross-functional feedback. Based on your organization's AI vision, are you making adequate progress? What else can or must be done to compete when your competitors and customers are using advanced AI?

Deploy an AI "Suggestion Box" that scans internal chatter and spots fresh ideas. Route each insight to the project owner and the senior sponsor. Skip the game of political telephone; direct feedback is clearer. Incentivize leaders to review and act on these signals often. Continually refine tactics to keep the octopus flexible.

3. Avoid Making AI an Imposition

AI adoption will get rocky. Some teams will resist or quietly shelve new tools. Mandates from above go only so far, and they can sap morale. Use a three-pronged approach instead:

- Explain why each process is changing and how you will measure success. Emphasize that AI augments staff skills.
- Let managers drive adoption within their own teams. Skip anonymous e-learning and one-off webinars and TED-style speeches from the C-suite. When possible, bring in external experts to speak so people gain perspective and confidence. Remember, change sticks the best when learning happens inside the squad, not when it's imposed from on high.
- Pick a transformation framework and follow it. AI adoption is an ongoing journey, not a one-time launch. Many firms use Kotter's eight-step model or Prosci's ADKAR (Awareness, Desire, Knowledge, Ability, Reinforcement) to guide change.

Culture shifts take more than well-written memos and declarations. Buy-in requires time and steady effort. Keep the AI dialogue alive with town halls, newsletters, training sessions, and pulse surveys. Gather feedback and continually adjust your message.

4. Set the Right Example

As we emphasized in Chapter 6, a positive, purposeful culture speeds AI adoption.

- Culture change starts with role models. Senior leaders must use data and AI daily. Employees spot such cues. When a predictive dashboard launches, watch the VPs. Do they quote it or rely on instinct?
- Your AI vision must guide choices, not just rest on slides.
- When projects stumble, repeat why the change matters. The vision may feel unnecessary in good times, but it anchors teams during weak results.
- Celebrate every win. Broadcast pilot milestones on internal channels. Praise the team, explain the steps, and link the benefits to the strategy. Discuss the tools second. Recognition fuels motivation and teaches peers.

Do all these things, and in time, staff will come to see AI as a potential helper. Skepticism will turn into curiosity: *Maybe AI can lift my work too.*

A FINAL WORD

One last lesson from the octopus: Don't copy its lifespan. As adaptable and enduring as the species is, each individual lives just a few years. They reproduce once, then die. Males expire after fertilization, and females starve to death while guarding their eggs. Even the Northern Giant Pacific Octopus, the Methuselah of the tribe, rarely reaches its fifth birthday.

Although the average public company's life shrank from about thirty-five years in 1970 to about twenty today, your organization needn't share that biological clock. Longevity is the result of successful strategic transformation. Hermès still crafts leather after 180 years, and W.R. Grace turned from harvesting Peruvian bird droppings in 1854 into a global chemical empire.

The coming AI wave will strip the shells from rigid incumbents. At the same time, generative AI's added value for the companies that adopt it will be in the trillions of dollars within a decade. For those who make the evolutionary leap, it may be the biggest opportunity of their lives.

Wire intelligence into every arm, push decision-making down from the C-suite and out to the customer-facing edges, and learn faster than the market shifts. Do that, and you will multiply your advantages for decades—perhaps centuries.

In the animal kingdom, natural selection is fate. In business, longevity is a result of choice. So choose adaptation. The new epoch has already begun.

APPENDIX

Scaling Enterprise AI

For many C-Suite leaders, scaling AI transformations at the enterprise level seems like an insurmountable challenge.

Despite all the hype, only about 26 percent of firms have seen "meaningful value" from their AI efforts.[65] Why is scaling AI so hard?

General Electric's (GE) early foray into algorithmic analytics tells the tale: In the mid-2010s, GE poured billions into a grand digital transformation vision centered on its Predix platform. The goal was to infuse AI-driven analytics into all of GE's industrial businesses. Externally, things looked promising. In 2014, GE announced over $1 billion in additional annual digital services revenue.[66] Internally, however, resources started to spread thin, projects lacked clear focus, and timelines slipped; trying to "boil the ocean" by transforming every unit simultaneously proved unmanageable. In 2017, Predix was broken apart and sold off as part of a companywide restructuring.

GE's stumble illustrates a sobering truth: Deep pockets and cutting-edge tech alone can't guarantee success in scaling automation if the technology lacks strategic focus and organizational alignment.

On the other hand, the rewards for getting it right are enormous. JPMorganChase, for example, deployed an AI system called COIN to review legal documents and loan agreements, work that had previously consumed 360,000 hours of lawyers' time annually.[67] COIN can parse those documents in seconds, freeing time for lawyers to focus on more complex, higher value work. COIN works because it was designed with a particular problem in mind, remains embedded within a very specific workstream, and focuses on tackling a high-volume, repetitive task. It avoided becoming a kind of "omnisolution."

Below, we offer suggestions for C-level executives, especially CIOs and CTOs, who are looking to sustainably scale AI.

BEGIN WITH PAIN POINTS, NOT TECHNOLOGY

Many enterprises launch dozens of AI pilots that never translate into business outcomes. Often, the issue is that the pilot wasn't intended to resolve a strategic challenge but to test a specific technical problem. Your organization will get far more out of its early AI experiments if they are framed as opportunities to resolve an actual problem for the business. Ask yourself:

▸ What use case is your pilot addressing?
▸ Does it solve for a real Job to be Done in a way that your customers will recognize?
▸ How might it be deployed if it were to succeed?

Pilots can sometimes be framed as low-stakes test runs, but the opposite perspective should be taken. AI pilots should be framed as an integral part of your organization's growth strategy.

DO LESS AND EXPECT MORE

Leading AI companies concentrate on fewer initiatives but anticipate roughly double the ROI compared to followers. Baking quantifiable metrics into early pilots can help your organization focus on those that seem most promising and can generate executive buy-in. Make the "right to scale" dependent on reaching predetermined benchmarks—for example, "if we can save at least 15 percent in costs through this supply chain routing tool, we can invest an additional X percent to implement it across logistics teams."

SOLIDIFY YOUR DATA FOUNDATIONS

The data that fuels your AI applications should be integrated, clean, and accessible. If your enterprise data is siloed across different systems, of poor quality, or hard to access, scaling AI across your enterprise will always be out of reach.

A crucial early step is creating a unified data platform—often a cloud-based data lake or warehouse—that aggregates relevant data from across the business. Airbus partnered with Palantir to build a platform called Skywise that pools data from its manufacturing and airline operations, enabling AI-powered predictive maintenance on aircraft. Starbucks realized that to personalize its offerings at scale, they needed to harness purchase and loyalty data from millions of customers in real time. To do so, they invested in a centralized analytics platform that pulls in transaction data, inventory levels, weather, and more. (Deep Brew from Chapter 5 also runs on this platform.) Getting these data flows established and making them accessible to AI models takes continual attention.

Cleaning and standardizing data can be a thankless task, but it is vital. Bosch, the German engineering giant, recognized that AI can only be as good as the data feeding it. It has made data governance a pillar of its strategy, ensuring that sensors on Bosch devices and machines feed consistent, accurate data into its AIoT (AI + IoT) systems. Bosch's vision is that by the end of 2025, all of its products will either contain AI or be made using AI—an audacious goal that required training 65,000 associates in AI and software practices to manage the data and development work.[68] By the beginning of 2025, Bosch staff had registered over 1,500 AI patents, making it a leading AI innovator in Europe. Bosch made data cleaning and standardization a concern for anyone responsible for designing and launching new offerings. If they had siloed that responsibility within a dedicated data engineering team, it would likely have led to little more than hole-plugging.

Accessible data is also key. If one department hoards data from another, they will impede cross-functional AI applications. Though there are legitimate privacy concerns, data siloing frequently stems from a political problem: a department trying to keep its "dirty laundry" out of sight.

To the extent possible, company data should be treated as a shared asset. Some leading firms adopt data catalogs or market-places internally, where teams can discover and request the datasets they need. Others create cross-department data squads to merge datasets for AI projects. The emergence of the "feature store" concept is one technical enabler here—a feature store is a centralized repository for ML features (data signals) that different models can reuse.[69] Implementing such data products can greatly speed scaling: For instance, if one team has engineered a useful feature (say, a customer lifetime value score), others can pull it from the store instead of reinventing the wheel. These stores also exist at the level of cloud providers such as AWS, and in company groups such as venture capital firm Prosus.[70]

IMPLEMENT MACHINE LEARNING OPS FOR LIFECYCLE MANAGEMENT

One-off AI solutions can be handcrafted; dozens cannot. This is where MLOps—a set of practices and tools to manage the machine learning lifecycle—comes in. MLOps is to AI models what DevOps is to software: it streamlines coding, testing, deployment, monitoring, and iteration. For instance, companies might use continuous integration/continuous deployment (CI/CD) pipelines for AI models, so that when data scientists commit a new model version, it automatically goes through tests and can be deployed to production in a governed way. MLOps platforms (such as open-source Kubeflow or commercial ones like Dataiku, Databricks MLflow, and Azure Machine Learning) can provide standard workflows for data prep, experiment tracking, model serving, and monitoring.

Netflix manages hundreds of ML models to power its recommendation engine, A/B testing, and content valuation. To keep track of these models, the company built a robust internal MLOps toolset around the open-source Metaflow platform to allow rapid experimentation and deployment. Uber took a similar path with its Michelangelo platform, which standardized the workflow for developing and deploying a model. These investments paid off by dramatically increasing the number of AI projects Uber could produce.

MAINTAIN SECURITY AND RELIABILITY

At scale, AI becomes part of mission-critical processes, so your cybersecurity infrastructure must be secure and robust. Incorporate AI systems into your cybersecurity threat models—AI introduces new risks like data poisoning (if someone maliciously feeds bad data to retrain a model) or adversarial inputs (specially crafted inputs that fool a model). Ensure proper access controls on data and models (who can deploy changes, who can view sensitive training data, etc.).

Also plan for fail-safes: If an AI service goes down or produces an outlier result, is there a human fallback or a simpler rule-based system? For example, if your AI-powered inventory optimization tool fails, can planners revert to a standard safety-stock formula until the tool is back? Where possible, high availability setups (redundant instances, etc.) should be considered for critical AI services.

Fundamentally, ensure that pilots address core business needs. Establish a method for prioritizing the AI use cases that seem most promising for your organization and double down on your investments in them. And, finally, establish the data infrastructure that will allow AI to scale from experiments to a streamlined and standardized process of continual improvement.

Over time, your organization's AI transformation will graduate from one-off, "artisanal" model-crafting to an assembly line of AI-driven solutions.

ABOUT THE AUTHORS

Jonathan Brill is the Futurist-in-Residence at Amazon, Head of Invention at Deepinvent.ai, Executive Chairman of the Center for Radical Change, and former Global Futurist and Research Director at HP. *Forbes* calls him "the world's leading futurist." As an AI Lab Chief, technology executive, and creative director at Frog Design, his teams have developed over 350 products, generating tens of billions of dollars in new revenue for clients. As a consultant, he has guided multinational corporations and national governments, as well as frontier tech firms working in AI, defense, food, and advanced manufacturing.

Stephen Wunker is the Managing Director of New Markets Advisors, a global consulting firm that develops growth strategies for innovators such as Meta and the Mayo Clinic. A pioneer in mobile marketing and payments, he led the development of one of the world's first smartphones. As a longtime collaborator with the late Clayton Christensen, Harvard Business School's legendary scholar of business disruption, Stephen played a key role in refining and applying his theories of Disruptive Innovation and Jobs to be Done. He has worked across sectors to help large organizations identify major opportunities and move quickly, despite legacy systems or cultural resistance.

ACKNOWLEDGMENTS

First, my thoughts go to Rebecca, Masha, Mom, Cathy, Margot and Lora—the ladies in my life.

It's been a pleasure to work on this book with so many friends, ranging from the whole crew at KPMG: Pär Edin, Brian Miske, Elisa Holland, Richard Entrup, David Pessah, Jenn Linardos. My secret technology cabinet: Kent Langley, David Andre, Ted Selker, Rodney Brooks, Deborah McGuinness and the other Deborah, Tommy Gardner and the many folks I can't mention across industries and government. My partner in global exploration, Niki Skene.

To Barbara Silva of Singularity Chile who, in 2019, made the first big bet on my research about AI and the future of organizations. To all of my amazing agents, in particular, Ellis Trevor at Chartwell, Barrett Cordero at BigSpeak, Angela Schelp at Executive Speakers, and Rainey Foster at Leading Authorities, and to Melissa Spencer as well as their entire organizations and to Tony D'Amelio for being there, advising me along this journey. This research would not have been possible without the thousands of executives your firms have put me in front of. These conversations have shaped my thinking on AI and organizations. To Steve Brown and Nik Badminton for always being there to chat on what they are seeing.

To Alvin Ho Young, Omar Acosta, Cary Janks, Patty Tulloch, Meghan Kennedy Cordella, Katie Burton and Chris West for helping me to clarify my thinking and always, always making me look great! To Arthur Goldwag, my life teacher and editor through the four years of birthing this book.

For the hard work on crunching the data, thank you to Michael McDonald at the Harrison Assessment and to Jim Povec for helping me make sense of it. Our intensive work studying the management traits of leaders who make better decisions under uncertainty has been transformational.

A special thanks to Adam Grant, Daniel Katsin, Gilad Karni and my mentor Robert Ellis for showing me, through their example, that a better way of living and leading is possible. I am also grateful for the insights of master coaches in my life. You always provide sage advice. In particular: Margaret Andrews of Harvard Business School, Ciela Hartanov of DropBox, Dorie Clark, Rita McGrath of Columbia Business School and Col. Mike Rauhut, Director of the Executive Coaching Program at the Army War College for guiding me through the soft side of radical change.

And to Steve Wunker. This journey began nearly a decade ago when I read your article. Thank you for answering my email asking questions about it and the so many that have come since. It was early evidence of what we have since quantified: that Strategic Serendipity is, in fact, the path to good fortune.

—Jonathan Brill

This may be my fifth book, but they don't get easier. In this case, we've written about a transformation that's just begun, and so we had to cobble together slices of the picture from a huge range of sources, making sure that the entire picture stayed coherent. We certainly needed help.

Thanks to Jonathan Brill in so many ways. The idea of the Octopus Organization stemmed from his speeches stretching back several years, and many of the concepts in this book came from his deep, creative analysis of what he's seeing on the frontlines of change. This book is different in many ways from my previous ones, and that's largely due to Jonathan's unique abilities and constant quest to look at old problems through new lenses.

I'm grateful as well to the many interviewees for this book. In particular, I appreciate the inputs from Andy Shin, Chief Strategy Officer at Mass General Brigham, and Mojgan Lefebvre, Chief Information and Operations Officer at Travelers. Both are practical visionaries who are at the forefront of these changes.

I'm also indebted to many collaborators. Several of my colleagues at New Markets Advisors commented on drafts. Among that team, Peter Hale was particularly instrumental in the work, researching theses, helping to construct arguments, and providing countless inputs into the text. Arthur Goldwag, a top-notch editor and writer, also worked extensively with us to brainstorm approaches, build out analogies, and craft the wording.

I owe many people who shaped the way I think, and none more than the late Clay Christensen. Clay mentored me for nearly six years with his firm, and he taught me how to think about disruptive innovations. AI may be the most disruptive innovation in history, and his lenses helped me take a systematic, organized view as to what it means.

Thanks as well to my family—Jessica, Wyatt, Cyrus, and Monty—who accompanied me on this journey. Wyatt's thinking about AI and leadership played an important role in Chapter 4 of this text. And thanks to my Dad, Robert Wunker, who as with each of my books gave it a detailed read and commentary.

This team was something of an Octopus Organization in itself, with true distributed intelligence. The output bears the authors' names, but it resulted from the efforts of many.

—Stephen Wunker

REFERENCES

INTRODUCTION

1. OpenAI et al., "Competitive Programming with Large Reasoning Models," arXiv, February 18, 2025, https://doi.org/10.48550/arXiv.2502 .06807.
2. See Mustafa Dogan, Alexandre Jacquillat, and Pinar Yildirim, "Strategic Automation and Decision-Making Authority," Journal of Economics & Management Strategy 33, no. 1 (September 2023): 203–46.

CHAPTER 1

3. See Jonathan Brill, Rogue Waves, 2021.
4. "AI Has High Data Center Energy Costs—but There Are Solutions | MIT Sloan," January 7, 2025.
5. "P&G Taps into AI and Automation for Faster, Smarter Operations," Consumer Goods Technology, December 3, 2024.
6. Qirui Hu, "Unilever's Practice on AI-Based Recruitment," Highlights in Business, Economics and Management 16 (2023): 256–63.
7. Ashish Vaswani et al., "Attention Is All You Need" (arXiv, August 2, 2023), https://doi.org/10.48550/arXiv.1706.03762; "Introducing ChatGPT," March 13, 2024, https://openai.com/index/chatgpt/.
8. "Smarter Claims Management, Smoother Settlements," Allianz.com, accessed June 17, 2025, https://www.allianz.com/en/mediacenter/news /articles/250205-smarter-claims-management-smoother-settlements .html.
9. "Siemens Drives AI Adoption with Industrial Operations X and NVIDIA . . . ," c2_ct_press_release, accessed June 17, 2025, https:// press.siemens.com/global/en/pressrelease/siemens-drives-ai-adoption -industrial-operations-x-and-nvidia-accelerated-industrial.
10. "Siemens and Qualcomm Technologies Set up the First Private Standal . . . ," c2_ct_press_release, accessed June 17, 2025, https://press .siemens.com/global/en/pressrelease/siemens-and-qualcomm-set-first -private-standalone-5g-network-industrial-environment.
11. "Dominion Resumes New Connections, But Loudoun Faces Lengthy Power Constraints | Data Center Frontier," accessed June 17, 2025, https://www.datacenterfrontier.com/energy/article/11436951/dominion- resumes-new-connections-but-loudoun-faces-lengthy-power-constraints.

12. "US Gas-Fired Turbine Wait Times as Much as Seven Years; Costs up Sharply," S&P Global Commodity Insights, May 20, 2025.

13. "Building Enterprise AI Maturity | MIT CISR," 2024.

14. Steve Blank, "Organizational Debt Is Like Technical Debt—But Worse," Forbes, May 18, 2015.

CHAPTER 2

15. Carl von Clausewitz, On War, trans. Michael Howard and Peter Paret (Princeton, New Jersey: Princeton University Press, 1984).

16. Alfonso Íñiguez, "The Octopus as a Model for Artificial Intelligence—A Multi-Agent Robotic Case Study:," in Proceedings of the 9th International Conference on Agents and Artificial Intelligence (9th International Conference on Agents and Artificial Intelligence, Porto, Portugal: SCITEPRESS - Science and Technology Publications, 2017), 439–44, https://doi.org/10.5220/0006125404390444.

17. "How Stripe Is Using AI to Create Personalized Checkout Experiences," March 26, 2025, https://stripe.com/blog/stripe-ai-personalized-checkout-experiences.

18. "Siemens, AWS Partner To Simplify Use Of AI In Software Development - Design Engineering," January 10, 2024, https://www.design-engineering.com/siemens-aws-partner-to-simplify-use-of-ai-in-software-development-1004041584/.

19. Slack, "How Beyond Better Foods Whips up Success with Slack and Salesforce," Slack, accessed April 4, 2025, https://slack.com/customer-stories/beyond-better-foods-story.

20. Bill Schaninger, Bryan Hancock, and Emily Field, Power to the Middle: Why Managers Hold the Keys to the Future of Work (Harvard Business Review Press, 2023).

21. Manuel Hoffman et al, "Generative AI and the Nature of Work," Harvard Business School Working paper 25-021, 2025.

22. Suqing Wu et al., "Human-Generative AI Collaboration Enhances Task Performance but Undermines Human's Intrinsic Motivation," Scientific Reports 15, no. 1 (April 29, 2025): 15105, https://doi.org/10.1038/s41598-025-98385-2; "How AI Will Divide the Best from the Rest," The Economist, accessed February 14, 2025, https://www.economist.com/finance-and-economics/2025/02/13/how-ai-will-divide-the-best-from-the-rest.

23. Agarwal, Nikhil, Alex Moehring, Pranav Rajpurkar, and Tobias Salz. Combining Human Expertise with Artificial Intelligence: Experimental Evidence from Radiology. NBER Working Paper Series, no. w31422. Cambridge, Mass: National Bureau of Economic Research, 2023.

24. Carlos Perez, The Deep Learning AI Playbook: Strategy for Disruptive Artificial Intelligence (Intuition Machine, 2017).

25. Francisco Castro, Jian Gao, and Sébastien Martin, "Does GenAI Impose a Creativity Tax?," MIT Sloan Management Review, October 31, 2024, https://sloanreview.mit.edu/article/does-genai-impose-a-creativity-tax/.

26. Stephen Wunker, "How AI Can Revolutionize Pharma Sales and Marketing," Forbes, June 5, 2023.
27. Alex Heath, "Mark Zuckerberg Says Meta Is Making This the 'Year of Efficiency,'" The Verge, February 2, 2023, https://www.theverge.com/2023/2/1/23581938/mark-zuckerberg-meta-earnings-q4-efficiency-cutting-managers.

CHAPTER 3
28. Sidney Carls-Diamante, "Where Is It Like to Be an Octopus?," Frontiers of Systems Neuroscience, March 13, 2022.
29. R. H. Coase, "The Nature of the Firm," Economica 4, no. 16 (1937): 386–405, https://doi.org/10.1111/j.1468-0335.1937.tb00002.x.
30. American Society of Landscape Architects, 2006: https://www.asla.org/awards/2006/studentawards/282.html.
31. Augusto Marietti, "API Mandate: How Jeff Bezos' Memo Changed Software Forever," Kong Inc., accessed March 13, 2025, https://konghq.com/blog/enterprise/api-mandate.

CHAPTER 4
32. Drucker Forum, 2024.
33. "IMD Future Readiness Indicator - CPG 2025," https://www.imd.org/future-readiness-indicator/home/consumer-packaged-goods-2025/.
34. Suqing Wu et al., "Human-Generative AI Collaboration Enhances Task Performance but Undermines Human's Intrinsic Motivation," Scientific Reports 15, no. 1 (April 29, 2025): 15105, https://doi.org/10.1038/s41598-025-98385-2.
35. "As AI's Power Grows, so Does Our Workday," CEPR, March 28, 2025, https://cepr.org/voxeu/columns/ais-power-grows-so-does-our-workday.
36. Jordi Canals and Franz Heukamp, The Future of Management in an AI World: Redefing Purpose and Strategy in the Fourth Industrial Revolution, Palgrave Macmillan IESE Business Collection (Palgrave Macmillan, 2020).
37. Alex Adamopoulos, "Opening Salvo: Radical (but Practical) Ideas for Advancing Knowledge Work" (16th Global Peter Drucker Forum, Vienna, 2024).
38. For Every Patient | Mass General Brigham. https://www.massgeneralbrigham.org/en/about/for-every-patient.
39. Andy Shin, Chief Strategy Officer at MGB, Interviewed by Stephen Wunker.

CHAPTER 5
40. Matthew A. Birk et al., "Temperature-Dependent RNA Editing in Octopus Extensively Recodes the Neural Proteome," Cell 186, no. 12 (June 8, 2023): 2544-2555.e13, https://doi.org/10.1016/j.cell.2023.05.004.

41. Robin Marantz Henig, "Experts Warned of a Pandemic Decades Ago. Why Weren't We Ready?," National Geographic, April 8, 2020, https://www.nationalgeographic.com/science/article/experts-warned-pandemic-decades-ago-why-not-ready-for-coronavirus.

42. Stephen Wunker, Jessica Wattman, and David Farber, Jobs to be Done: A Roadmap for Customer-Centered Innovation, 2016.

43. For more on when to fast follow, see Stephen's article "Better Growth Decisions: Early Mover, Fast Follower, or Late Follower," Strategy & Leadership 40, no. s (2012), doi:10.1108/10878571211209341.

CHAPTER 6

44. Sy Montgomery, The Soul of an Octopus: A Surprising Exploration into the Wonder of Consciousness (Atria Books, 2015).

45. See, for instance, Jennifer Mather, "The Case for Octopus Consciousness: Valence," NeuroSci 3, no. 4 (2022), 656–66; https://doi.org/10.3390/neurosci3040047.

46. John P. Kotter, Leading Change, 1st ed. (Harvard Business School Press, 1996).

47. Clayton M. Christensen and Michael E. Raynor, The Innovator's Solution: Creating and Sustaining Successful Growth, 1st ed. (Boston: Harvard Business School Press, 2003).

48. John P. Kotter, Leading Change, 1st ed. (Harvard Business School Press, 1996).

49. "IBM Slashes around 8,000 Jobs, Primarily from Its HR Division," ETHRWorld Southeast Asia, May 27, 2025, The Economic Times, https://hrsea.economictimes.indiatimes.com/news/industry/ibm-lays-off-8000-workers-in-major-hr-restructuring-driven-by-ai/121405057.

50. Trey Williams, "Overlooking High Performers Can Be a Costly Mistake, Fortune," March 18, 2024, https://fortune.com/2024/03/18/overlooking-high-performing-workers-costly-mistake-management/.

51. See a book that Stephen assisted on early in his career: Jay W. Lorsch and Tom J. Tierney, Aligning the Stars: How to Succeed When Professionals Drive Results (Harvard Business Review Press, 2002).

52. Stephen Wunker, Jennifer Luo Law, and Hari Nair, The Innovative Leader: Step-By-Step Lessons from Top Innovators for You and Your Organization (Morgan James Publishing, 2024).

CHAPTER 7

53. Wunker, Law, and Nair, The Innovative Leader, 2024.

54. MM Filkowski, RN Cochran, and BW Haas, "Altruistic Behavior: Mapping Responses in the Brain," Neuroscience and Neuroeconomics, 2016

55. Amy C. Edmondson, "Opening Salvo: Radical (but Practical) Ideas for Advancing Knowledge Work," 16th Global Peter Drucker Forum, Vienna, 2024.

56. Mark Granovetter, "The Strength of Weak Ties," The American Journal of Sociology 78, no. 6 (May 1973): 1360–80, https://doi.org/10.1086 /225469.

57. Dena Levitz, "6 Principles Clark Gilbert Used to Transform Deseret News," American Press Institute (blog), February 1, 2013, https:// americanpressinstitute.org/6-principles-clark-gilbert-used-transform -deseret-news/.

58. Roger Martin, "Strategy & Design Thinking," Medium (blog), July 16, 2021, https://rogermartin.medium.com/strategy-design-thinking -faf6b787160b.

59. Zachary Skidmore, "DOE: Nuclear Energy Needs to Triple by 2050, AI and Data Centers Drive Demand," DCD, October 7, 2024, https://www .datacenterdynamics.com/en/news/doe-report-highlights-need-to-triple -nuclear-capacity-by-2050-due-to-ai-and-data-center-load-growth/ ?utm_source=chatgpt.com; U.S. Department of Energy, "Pathways to Commercial Liftoff Reports," accessed July 7, 2025, https://www.energy .gov/lpo/pathways-commercial-liftoff-reports.

60. "AI Adoption Statistics 2024: All Figures & Facts to Know," Vention, https://ventionteams.com/solutions/ai/adoption-statistics.

61. Kate Den Houter, "AI in the Workplace: Answering 3 Big Questions," Gallup, October 8, 2024, https://www.gallup.com/workplace/651203 /workplace-answering-big-questions.aspx.

CHAPTER 8

62. Quoted in Ceri Parker, "Artificial Intelligence Could Be Our Saviour, According to the CEO of Google," World Economic Forum, January 24, 2018, https://www.weforum.org/stories/2018/01/google-ceo-ai-will-be -bigger-than-electricity-or-fire/.

63. Randall Stross, "Failing Like a Buggy Whip Maker? Better Check Your Simile," The New York Times, January 9, 2010, sec. Business, https:// www.nytimes.com/2010/01/10/business/10digi.html.

64. Yijia Shao et al., "Future of Work with AI Agents: Auditing Automation and Augmentation Potential Across the U.S. Workforce," Future of Work with AI Agents, Stanford University SALT Lab, accessed June 19, 2025, https://futureofwork.saltlab.stanford.edu/.

APPENDIX

65. "AI Adoption in 2024: 74% of Companies Struggle to Achieve and Scale Value," BCG Global, October 24, 2024, https://www.bcg.com /press/24october2024-ai-adoption-in-2024-74-of-companies-struggle-to -achieve-and-scale-value.

66. "GE to Open Up Predix Industrial Internet Platform to All Users," press release, General Electric, October 9, 2014, https://www.ge.com/news /press-releases/ge-open-predix-industrial-internet-platform-all-users.

67. Adnan Masood, "AI in Organizational Change Management—Case Studies, Best Practices, Ethical Implications, and Future Technological

Trajectories," Medium (blog), June 1, 2025, https://medium.com/@adnanmasood/ai-in-organizational-change-management-case-studies-best-practices-ethical-implications-and-179be4ec2583.

68. "Bosch Uses Software and AI to Make Its Products Smarter and Make People's Lives Safer," press release, Bosch Media Service, January 6, 2025, https://us.bosch-press.com/pressportal/us/en/press-release-26240.html.

69. "Introduction to Feature Management in Vertex AI," Google Cloud, accessed June 10, 2025, https://cloud.google.com/vertex-ai/docs/featurestore.

70. Stephen Wunker, "How to Build AI Capabilities Across an Enterprise," Forbes, February 22, 2024, https://www.forbes.com/sites/stephenwunker/2024/02/22/how-to-build-ai-capabilities-across-an-enterprise/.

INDEX

Abductive reasoning, 100

Accessible data, 44, 122

Accuracy gains, 114

Acquaintances, weak ties to, 97

Adamopoulos, Alex, 59

Adaptation:
    to AI use, 5
    for longevity, 118
    (*See also* Sensing-based
        adaptation)

ADAR enzyme, 67

ADKAR (Awareness, Desire,
    Knowledge, Ability,
    Reinforcement) model, 117

Adoption metrics, 114

Adversarial inputs, 123

Afførd case example:
    AI transformation, 18–19
    culture change, 89–90
    data transparency, 51
    distributed decision-making,
        38–39
    leadership styles, 64–65
    sensing-based adaptation, 77–78
    weighing of alternatives, 108

Agency, human, 113

Agentic AI and AI agents, 77
    at Afførd, 77
    capabilities of, viii–ix
    distributed decision-making with,
        26–27
    interactions between, 12, 13
    performance of radiologists
        working with, 32
    sensing-based adaptation with,
        44

trusting, but verifying
    information from, 96
    in "T-Town Treats" example, 4–5

AGI (artificial general intelligence),
    43

Agile Heart (leadership style):
    at Afførd, 65
    balancing Analytic Heart and, 54
    described, 54
    at Mass General Brigham, 62–63
    situations requiring, 56–58, 116
    at Walmart Data Ventures, 58

Agile operations, 25, 75–77

AI (*see* Artificial intelligence)

AI agents (*see* Agentic AI and AI
    agents)

AI ambassador network, 112

AI assistants:
    frictionless information from, 43
    meeting notes from, 9
    network map audit with, 97
    for primary care physicians,
        63–64
    in "T-Town Treats" case example,
        4

AI champions, finding, 112

AI governance framework, 115

AI literacy training, 61, 112

AI Suggestion Box, 116

AI transformation, viii
    at Afførd, 18–19
    authors' expertise guiding, xi–xii
    bottom-up, 28–30
    culture necessary for, 84–85
    culture of shared ownership over,
        108

AI transformation (*continued*)
  enterprise-level, 119–124
  fear of, 82
  holistic, systemic changes in use
    of technology for, 105–106
  key problems with, xii
  Octopus Organization approach
    to, x–xi, 19
  overview of, xiii–xv
  systemic change for, 105–106
  technological gates on, 13–16
  timing your organization's,
    10–16
  vision of the future for, 16–17
  wait-and-see approach to, x
AIoT systems, at Bosch, 121
Airbus, 121
Airtable, 43
Aligned Heart (leadership style):
  at Afførd, 65
  described, 54
  enhancing job satisfaction for
    workers, 58–61
  at Mass General Brigham, 62, 63
  situations calling for, 58–61, 116
  using empathy and intuition, 60
Allianz, 13
Alternatives, defining and
  weighing, 108
Altruism, 93, 94
Altshuller, Genrich, 48
Amazon, xi
  as AI early mover, 106
  in Covid crisis, 69, 70
  data transparency at, 50
  leadership principles of, 110, 111
  transaction costs for, 45
  vibe coding at, 11
Amazon Web Services (AWS):
  AI platform for frontline
    empowerment by, 29–30
  feature stores of, 122
  as hyperscaler, 14
  software development at, 50
Ammonite:
  dominance and extinction of, vii,
    ix, 98

failure of, to adapt, 75, 106
gradual evolution of, vii, viii, 68
Analysis paralysis, 47
Analytic Heart (leadership style):
  at Afførd, 64–66
  balancing Agile Heart and, 54
  described, 54
  at Mass General Brigham, 62
  situations requiring, 55–56, 116
Android platform, 73
Annual planning cycles, 77
Apple, 73
Application programming interfaces
  (APIs), 11, 26–27, 50
Artificial general intelligence
  (AGI), 43
Artificial intelligence (AI):
  to amplify human coordination,
    ix
  changes in use of, 105–106
  as competitive necessity, 8–10
  experimentation with vs.
    integration of, x
  exponential evolution of, viii–x
  fear of, 82
  generative, 59, 92, 118
  human adaptation to, 5
  and internal jobs to be done,
    35–36
  measuring impact of, 61
  number and ROI of initiatives
    involving, 120–121
  organizational growth enabled by,
    8–10
  pathway for using, x–xi
  and physician performance, 32
  putting boundaries around, 35
  reimagining of organizational
    growth with, 8–10
  reinvention of organizational
    structure by, 4–5
  software maturity, 13, 16
  as sole driver of transformation,
    105
  technological gates for, 13–16
  transformation driven by (*see* AI
    transformation)

understanding strategy in context of, 107–108
(*See also entries beginning* AI)
Artificial superintelligence (ASI), ix, 10, 43
ASI (*see* Artificial superintelligence)
Auftragstaktik, 24
Automation:
  and Aligned Heart, 59–60
  in bottom-up AI transformation, 28–29
  reducing coordination costs with, 45
  workforce reduction due to, 83
Awareness, Desire, Knowledge, Ability, Reinforcement (ADKAR) model, 117
AWS (*see* Amazon Web Services)
Azure Machine Learning, 123

bbbaaahhhhh (Reddit user), 43
Benchmarks, for pilot initiatives, 120–121
Beyond Better Foods, 30
Biases:
  at legacy and highly regulated firms, 17
  against novel ideas, 100
  using AI to check for, 49
  against working with AI, 32
Big-picture thinking, 17
BlackBerry, 74
Bosch, 121
Bottom-up AI transformation, 28–30
Bottom-up feedback loops, 72
Boundaries:
  around artificial intelligence, 35
  translating context across, 75
Brill, Jonathan, xi
Buggy whip makers, 106–107
Business ecosystem, attending to, 45–46
Business processes:
  at industrial organizations, 54
  quality control for, 56

sensing-based adaptation of, 67–68

Canals, Jordi, 59
Cancer detection, 9–10
Capabilities, repurposing, 106–107
Capital constraints, 6–7
Card counting, 92, 93
Carls-Diamante, Sidney, 41
Casinos, improving luck in, 92, 93
Celebrating wins, 117
"Centaurs," 14
Center for Radical Change, xi
Centers of Excellence, at MGB, 62
Centralized decision making, 23–25
Chance, defined, 91
Change management:
  for AI adoption, 61
  overseeing, 115–118
  in response to disruption, 98
Chaos, controlling, 98–99
Chaos compass, 99
Chatbots, x, 109
ChatGPT, viii
  critical thinking and using, 32
  debut of, xii, 13
  octopus poetry from, 67
  public data used by, 12
Chorus, 33–34
Christensen, Clayton, xi–xii, 35, 82
CI/CD (continuous integration/continuous deployment) pipelines, 122
Clausewitz, Carl von, 24
Clean data, 121–122
Clinical Trials Office, at MGB, 62
Coase, Ronald, 45
Cognitive biases (*see* Biases)
Cognitive sloth, 32
COIN system, 119–120
Collaboration:
  after AI transformation, 30
  with artificial intelligence, 55
  leveraging help and, 95–96
  and strategic serendipity, 91, 93
Collective emotions, 82
Collective intelligence, 75

Communication:
    about vision, 110
    of change rationale, 117
    democratization of, 43–45
    quantity and quality of, 25
    of success metrics, 117
    transparent, 61
Community building, 93
Competence, asking for help and, 95
Compliance outcomes of
    experiments, 114
Connection brokering, 97
Connections, using, 96–97
Consultant, AI as, 55
Contacts, lapsed, 97
Context of procedures, 73–75
Continuous dashboards, 51
Continuous delivery, 25
Continuous integration/continuous
    deployment (CI/CD) pipelines,
    122
Continuous learning, 61
Continuous quality monitoring, 8
Controlling chaos, in LUCK
    framework, 98–99
Cooperation, 91
Coordination:
    AI to amplify, ix
    in neural necklace, 41–42
Coordination costs, 45
Copilot, 11
Covid crisis, 68–70, 72
Creativity, 33
Crises, opportunities in, 69
Critical thinking skills:
    AI use and, 32–33, 49, 51, 56
    of leaders, 32–33
Cross-departmental data squads,
    122
Cross-functional feedback, 116
C-suite leaders (see Senior
    executives)
Culture change, xiv, 81–90
    at Afførd, 89–90
    buy-in on, 117
    DAOs and HFT firms as models
        of, 84–85

and emotionally-driven resistance
    to change, 82–84
and function of emotions for
    octopuses, 81–82
ingredients of, 85–86
pace of, 14, 16
at Princess Cruises, 87–89
surveying employees about need
    for, 85
transformation plan on, 115–118
Cunningham, Ward, 99–100
Curiosity, 97, 100
Customer insights, 71, 77–78
Customization, AI for, 76
Cybersecurity, 123–124

Daily pulse, 99
DAOs (decentralized autonomous
    organizations), 84
Dashboards, continuous, 51
Data:
    for enterprise-level AI
        transformation, 121–122
    seeing white spaces in, 99
Data catalogs, 122
Data centers, 7, 14, 16, 101
Data governance, 121
Data infrastructure, 123–124
Data lakes, 11
Data marketplaces, 122
Data poisoning, 123
Data transparency, xiii, 41–52
    at Afførd, 51
    at Amazon, 50
    avoiding pitfalls of, 46–47
    for intelligence everywhere
        and mission-specific focus,
        42–43
    neural necklace of octopus as
        model for, 41–42
    in Penny Post system, 43–45
    preparing staff for increasing,
        47–49
Databricks MLflow, 123
Dataiku, 123
Data-to-product pipeline, 56–57
De Mestral, George, 97

Decentralized autonomous
organizations (DAOs), 84
Decision making:
about experimentation program,
114
about transformation plan, 108
charting/mapping, 35, 109
influence of organizational
structure on, 24–25
speed of, 49
visibility of impact of, 4
(*See also* Distributed
decision-making)
Deep Brew platform, 72, 121
Deepinvent, 11, 76
DeepMind, 11
DeepSeek, viii
Democratization:
of access to information, 75 (*See
also* Data transparency)
of communication, 43–45
Devil's Advocate Unit, Israeli
Military Intelligence
Directorate, 49
Digital Clinical Research
Organization, 63
Digital pathology, 9–10
Disruptive innovation theory, xii
Distributed decision-making, xiii,
23–40, 77
at Afførd, 38–39
for bottom-up AI transformation,
28–30
impact of, on middle managers'
role, 30–35
and influence of organizational
structure on decision making,
24–25
leadership of switch to, 34–35
nine brains of octopus as model
for, 23
by Prussian army, 23–24
to reduce organizational debt,
15
tactics for, 25–27
at Travelers Insurance, 37–38
Distributed insights, 42–43

Dockwra, William, 44
Dominion Energy, 14
Drucker, Peter, 47, 91

Ebola outbreak, 69
Edge computing, 13, 16
"Edge" customer-facing managers,
85–86
Edison, Thomas, 105
Edmondson, Amy, 95–96
Efficiency gains, 114
Efficiency metrics, 47
Einstein, Albert, 100–101
Electricity, 105–106
Emergn, 59
Emory University, 59
Emotions:
of octopuses, 81–82
resistance to change driven by,
82–84
Employees:
generative AI and engagement
of, 59
preparing, for increased data
transparency, 47–49
surveying, on need for culture
change, 85
understanding needs of, 60
Energy systems, 7
Enterprise-level AI transformation,
119–124
current level of, 14
cybersecurity and reliability for,
123–124
data required for, 121–122
at GE vs. JPMorgan Chase,
119–120
MLOps for, 122–123
number and ROI of initiatives in,
120–121
pilots that address pain points in,
120
Environmental impact, of extractive
resource use, 101
Ethan Allen, 18
Europe, army strategy in, 23–24
Executive bauble problem, 28

Experimentation:
  for culture change, 86
  designing and launching program
    for, 113–115
  five-step process for, 76–77
  initial test beds for, 113
  at Princess Cruises, 87–88
  for technology change, 87–89
  (*See also* Pilot initiatives and
    projects)
Extractive resource use, 101

Fail-safes, for AI services, 123
Failure, premortem worksheet
    imagining, 100
Fear, 81, 82
Feature stores, 122
Feedback:
  bottom-up, 72
  on culture change, 116, 117
  in industrial organizations, 4
  psychological safety and, 61
First mover advantage, 73, 106
First principles canvas, 100
5G networks, private, 14, 16
"Focus on what you can control"
    approach, 16
For Every Patient initiative, 63
Forbes, xi
Ford, Henry, 106
Foresight, 70
Frictionless information, 46–47
Frog Design, xi
Front-line personnel, problem
    solving by, 26 (*See also*
    Distributed decision-making)
Fukushima nuclear disaster (2011),
    69–70

G7 nations, working-age population
    in, 6
Gas turbines, 14
Gemini, viii
General Electric (GE), 119
Generative AI, 59, 92, 118
Geopolitical turbulence, 7
Gilbert, Clark, 98

Glassdoor, 59
Gong, 33–34
Google, 106
Governance framework, 115
Granovetter, Mark, 97
Grok, viii
Groupthink, 47
Growth, 3–10
  AI-enabled, xiii, 8–10
  organizational structure and, 3–5
  trends disrupting industrial
    organizations', 5–7
Gut instincts, 56

Haim's law, 49
The Handbook of Social Psychology,
    sixth ed. (Gilbert et al.), 95
Harrison Assessment, 93
Harvard Business School, xi–xii,
    30–31
Help, leveraging, 95–96
Hermès, 106–107, 118
Hermès, Emile-Maurice, 106–107
Hewlett Packard Enterprise, 73
HFT firms (high-frequency
    trading) firms, 84–85
Hierarchical organizations:
  AI's challenges to, x
  extinction for rigid, ix
  incremental change at, viii
  railroads as, 4
  top-down transformations at, 28
High-frequency trading (HFT)
    firms, 84–85
Highly regulated firms, 17, 110
High-performing staff,
    transitioning, 83–84
HP, xi, 73, 82
Huang, Jensen, 3
Hub-and-spoke management
    system, 3–4
Human resources (HR) team:
  screening systems used by, 9
  support for AI transition in, 109
Hyperscalers, 14
Hypotheses, creating and testing,
    76

IBM, 83–84
IESE, 59
IKEA, 18
Industrial networks, private, 14, 16
Industrial organizations:
  employee input at, 95–96
  hub-and-spoke management
    system of, 3–4
  rigid processes and architectures
    of, 54
  trends disrupting growth of, 5–7
Infrastructure:
  cybersecurity, 123
  data, 123 124
  to support AI transformation, 7,
    115
In-Home Usage Tests, Scintilla, 58
Iñiguez, Santiago, 97
Innovator MESH Network, 62
Input, asking for, 96
Insights, synthesis of, 11–12
Inspiring others, 60
Instincts, 56
Institutional velocity, 14, 16
Insurance Copilot, 13
Integrated data, 121
Intelligence, sharing, 75
Intelligence everywhere, 27, 42–43,
  77
Intelligent rule-breaking, 75
Internal entrepreneurs, of culture
  change, 86
Internet, 8, 98
Introverts, drawing out, 97
Investments:
  estimating, for AI transformation,
    109
  evaluating suitability of, 76
iPad, 73
Israeli Military Intelligence
  Directorate, 49
Iteration, encouraging, 116

Job satisfaction, 58–61
Jobs to Be Done:
  optimizing organization by
    considering internal, 35–36

satisfying customers'
  unrecognized, 99
understanding customers', 71, 76
Wunker's theory of, xii
Jobs to be Done (Wunker), 35
JPMorgan Chase, 119
Judgment:
  about data collection and
    distribution, 46
  at industrial organizations, 4
  of middle managers, 31–33

Key performance indicators (KPIs):
  for experimentation program, 114
  overfocusing on, 16
  of productivity, 46–47
Keystroke trackers, 46–47
Klibanski, Anne, 63
Knowing what's missing, in LUCK
  framework, 99–100
Knowledge categories, 71–73, 76
Knowledge management systems,
  37–38, 43, 109
Known Knowns, 71, 72
Known Unknowns, 71, 72
Kotter, John, 82, 83, 117
KPIs (*see* Key performance indicators)
Kubeflow, 122

Labor scarcity, 6
LakehouseIQ platform, 11
Lapsed contacts, reaching out to, 97
Large language models (LLMs),
  26, 37
L&D (learning and development)
  team, support for, 109
Leadership styles, xiii
  at Afførd, 64–65
  Agile Heart, 56–58
  Aligned Heart, 58–61
  Analytic Heart, 55–56
  establishing, 116
  at Mass General Brigham, 62–64
  shifting between, 54
  three hearts of octopus as model
    for, 53
  at Walmart Data Ventures, 58

Learning:
  continuous, 61
  from success and failures, 57
Learning and development (L&D)
  team, support for, 109
Lefebvre, Mojgan, 37, 112
Legacy firms, biases of, 17
Leveraging help, in LUCK
  framework, 95–96
LinkedIn, 97
London, England, Penny Post in,
  43–45
L'Oréal, 56–57
Loudoun County, Va., data center
  hookups in, 14
Luck, xiv, 91–102
  defined, 91
  as factor in octopus's survival, 91
  humans' ability to enhance/
    increase, 91–92
  preparation to capitalize on,
    92–93
  serendipity and, 92
  types of, 94
LUCK framework of behaviors,
  94–101
  about, 94
  controlling chaos, 98–99
  knowing what's missing, 99–100
  leveraging help, 95–96
  putting, into practice, 100–101
  using connections, 96–97
Luddites, 82

Machine learning operations
  (MLOps), 122–123
Machinery operators, decision
  making by, 38
Management styles (see Leadership
  styles)
Managers:
  as culture change champions,
    85–86
  as drivers of AI adoption, 117
  "edge" customer-facing, 85–86
  LUCK behaviors of, 93–100
  management metrics for, 114

  resistance to transformation from,
    83
  sales, 33–34
  (See also Middle managers)
Mandated AI adoption, 116–117
Marketing teams, decision making
  by, 39
Martin, Roger, 98
Mass extinction event, vii–viii, 45
Mass General Brigham (MGB),
  62–64
Mass General Brigham Ventures,
  63
Mass-mailings, customizing, 44
McGrath, Rita, 56
MCPs (model context protocols),
  11
Meaningful work, 60–61
Mendelson, Haim, 49
Mentoring, reverse, 96
Meta, 34, 106
Metaflow platform, 123
MGB (Mass General Brigham),
  62–64
Michelangelo platform, 123
Microsoft:
  data integration by, 11
  digital assistants, 9
  HP as follower of, 73
  successful transformation at, 83
  work charts at, 36
Microsoft 365, AI search features,
  43
Middle managers:
  as AI champions, 112
  alignment meetings for, 9
  as culture change champions,
    85–86
  impact of distributed decision-
    making on, 27, 30–35
Milestones, for change, 110, 117
Missed opportunities, seizing,
  99–100
Mission tactics, 24
Mission-specific focus, 42–43
MLOps (machine learning
  operations), 122–123

Model context protocols (MCPs), 11
ModiFace, 56
Montgomery, Sy, 81

Nadella, Satya, 83
Napoleonic Wars, 24
Nash, Ogden, 23
The Nature of the Firm (Coase), 45
Netflix, 123
Network map audit, 97
Networking, 96–97
New Markets Advisors, xi
New perspectives, gaining, 99–100
Newspapers, impact of internet on,
 98
Ninth International Conference
 on Agents and Artificial
 Intelligence, 27
Northern Giant Pacific Octopus,
 118
Notion, 43
Nuremberg Automotive Test
 Center, 14
NVIDIA, 13

OCS (Optimized Checkout Suite),
 29
October 7, 2023 attacks, 72
Octopus:
 adaptability of, 75
 emotions of, 81–82
 lifespan of, 118
 luck as factor in survival of, 91
 as model for AI-enabled
  organization (*see* Octopus
  Organization(s))
 neural necklace of, 41–42
 nine brains of, 23, 27, 42
 pace of transformation for, 13
 resilience of, vii–viii, 67
 sensing by, 70
 three hearts of, 53
"The Octopus" (Nash), 23
*The Octopus as a Model for Artificial
 Intelligence* (Ninth International
 Conference on Agents and
 Artificial Intelligence), 27

"An Octopus Has Three Whole
 Hearts" (Sullivan), 53
Octopus Organization(s):
 approach to AI transformation
  at, x–xi, 19
 culture change at, 81–90
 data transparency at, 41–52
 distributed decision-making at,
  23–40
 leadership styles at, 53–66
 middle managers in, 31
 plan for becoming (*see*
  Transformation plan)
 sensing-based adaptation for,
  67–78
OneDrive, 11
Open interfaces, at Amazon, 49
Opportunities:
 assessment of potential, 57
 controlling chaos to identify, 98
 in crises, 69
 feedback loops to identify, 73
 seizing missed, 99–100
 sensing, 70
Optimized Checkout Suite (OCS),
 29
Organization readiness, for
 transformation, 109
Organizational change:
 communicating rationale for,
  117
 emotionally-driven resistance to,
  82–84
 preparing for, 111–113
 (*See also* Change management;
  Culture change)
Organizational culture:
 and Aligned Heart, 58–60
 of shared ownership over
  transformation, 108
 stating rules of, 84–85
 that reward curiosity, 100
Organizational debt, 15, 16
Organizational structure:
 AI's reinvention of, xii, 4–5
 flattening of, 34–35, 54
 and growth, 3–5

Organizational structure (*continued*)
influence of, on decision making,
24–25
middle managers' role in
changing, 11
reducing organizational debt by
changing, 15
sensing-based adaptation of,
67–68
(*See also* Hierarchical
organizations)
Otter, 9
Outlook Teams, 11

Pain points, addressing, 87, 120
Palantir, 121
Palm, 73
Pasteur, Louis, 92
PDA (personal digital assistant), 74
Peer review, 100
Penny Post system, 43–45
Performance metrics, focusing on,
16–17 (*See also* Key performance
indicators (KPIs))
Permission barriers, between AI
systems, 75
Personal digital assistant (PDA), 74
P&G (Procter & Gamble), 8, 71
Pichai, Sundar, 105
Pilot initiatives and projects:
addressing pain points in, 120
core business needs as guide for,
123
for culture change, 85, 86
disciplined experimentation with,
113–114
at Mass General Brigham, 63–64
number of and ROI for, 120–121
for organizational transformation,
xii
Planning meetings, 108
Playgrounds, risk bands in, 48–49
Portfolio management system,
76–77
Portfolio strategy, 57
Postmortem worksheets, 100
Power grid expansion, 7, 14, 16

Predix platform, 119
Preparation, to capitalize on luck,
92–93
Primary care physicians, AI
assistants for, 63–64
Princess Cruises, 87–89
Prioritization, of initiatives, 108, 123
Private 5G and industrial networks,
14, 16
Procedures, syntax vs. context of,
73–75
Process quality control, 56
Process simulation, 12
Procter & Gamble (P&G), 8, 71
Procurement staff, decision-making
by, 39
Productivity metrics, 46–47
Project planning, 12
Prosci, 117
Prosus, 122
Protectionism, 7
Prussian army, 23–24
Psion PLC, 74, 82
Psychological safety, 56, 61, 95
Public companies, longevity of, 118
Public ritual, of asking for help, 96

Qualcomm, 14
Quality gains, 114

Radiologists performance, AI's
effects on, 32
Railroads, 3–4, 54
Reasoning, abductive, 100
Recognition, 117
Red team drills, 99
Reframing chaos, 98
Reliability, of AI service, 123–124
Resilience, vii–viii, 67
Resistance to change:
emotionally-driven, 82–84
overcoming, 116–117
Resynchronization, 26
Return on investment (ROI), pilot
initiative, 120–121
Reverse mentoring, 96
Risk and return analysis, 76

Risk bands, 48–49, 55
Risk outcomes, of experiments, 114
Robotic systems, AI-driven, 27
ROI (return on investment), pilot
    initiative, 120–121
Role modeling:
    of asking for help, 96
    for culture change, 85, 86, 117

Safety, psychological, 56, 61, 95
Sales managers, 33–34
Sales representatives, 34
SARS outbreak, 69
Scaling up concepts, 57 (*See
    also* Enterprise-level AI
    transformation)
Scarcity mindset, 94
Scintilla, 58
Search features, AI, 43, 77–78
Self-driving cars, viii
Senior executives:
    as AI champions, 112
    as culture change champions,
        85–86
    distributed decision-making led
        by, 34–35
    fear of transformation for, 83
    foresight of, 33
    impact of distributed decision-
        making on, 26, 27, 39
    limiting control of, 116
Sensing-based adaptation, xiii,
    67–78
    at Afførd, 77–78
    Agile operations for, 75–77
    and AI tools for sensing, 70
    in Covid crisis, 68–70
    involving customer insights, 71,
        77–78
    knowledge categories for, 71–73
    of processes and structures, 67–68
    RNA-powered resilience of
        octopus as model for, 67
    and syntax vs. context of
        procedures, 73–75
September 11, 2001 terrorist attack,
    72

Serendip, 92
Serendipity, strategic, 89, 91–93, 98
    (*See also* LUCK framework of
    behavior)
Service interfaces, at Amazon, 49
Service-as-software paradigm,
    viii–ix
Shared ownership:
    of AI transformation, 108
    of data, 122
Shared sense of purpose, 59–60
SharePoint, 11
Shin, Andy, 63–64
Siemens:
    AI platform for frontline
        empowerment by, 29–30
    industrial computers from, 13
    labor scarcity at, 6
    private 5G network installation,
        14
Siloed information, 51, 95, 121,
    122
Skill development, 31, 61
Skills gaps, 111, 114
Skywise platform, 121
Slack, 43
Social and Language Technologies
    Lab, 113
SOPs (standard operating
    procedures), 6, 73–75
The Soul of an Octopus
    (Montgomery), 81
S&P Global, 14
Specialists, as AI champions, 112
Sri Lanka, 92
Stalin, Joseph, 48
Standard operating procedures
    (SOPs), 6, 73–75
Standardization:
    data, 121–122
    of workflows, with MLOps,
        122–123
Stanford University, 49, 113
Starbucks, 72, 121
Strategic serendipity, 89, 91–93, 98
    (*See also* LUCK framework of
    behavior)

Strategy:
  AI experiments that drive, 113
  in context of AI, 107–108
  pilot projects' alignment with, 120
Stress-testing plans, 99
Stripe, 29
Success metrics:
  communicating, 117
  for experimentation program,
    114–115
  identifying, 109
  for pilot initiatives, 120–121
  tracking, 116
Sullivan, Joy, 53
Supply chain management, 38–39,
  71
Support infrastructure, building,
  7, 115
Syntax, of procedures, 73–74
Systemic change, for AI
  transformation, 105–106

Talent plan, 111–112
Technology:
  experiments to change, 87–89
  and organizational structure,
    24–25
  resistance to using, 82
Telegraph:
  organizational structure dictated
    by, 24, 25
  railroads and, 3–5
  von Moltke's misgivings about,
    25, 27
Theory of Innovative Problem
  Solving (TRIZ), 48
Theory of mind, 42
Threats, sensing and assessing, 57,
  70
"The Three Princes of Serendip"
  (folktale), 92
Timeline, for realizing AI vision,
  110
Timing, of AI transformation,
  10–16
Top-down organizations (see
  Hierarchical organizations)

Toyota, 69–70
Trade Desk, 45–46
Training:
  AI literacy, 61, 112
  for culture change, 85, 86
  metrics for, 114
Transaction costs, 45
Transformation:
  AI-driven (see AI transformation)
  failed vs. successful, 82–83
  frameworks for, 117
  for survival, of octopuses, 106
  survival threats as drivers of, vii–ix
Transformation plan, xiv, 105–118
  at Amazon, 111
  building support infrastructure,
    115
  defining the vision, 107–110
  designing and launching an
    experimentation program,
    113–115
  at Hermès, 106–107
  overseeing change management,
    115–118
  preparing the organization for
    change, 111–113
Transformer models, 13, 92
Transparent communication, 61
Travelers Insurance, 37–38, 43, 112
Trend-sensing, 57
TrendSpotter, L'Oréal, 56
TRIZ (Theory of Innovative
  Problem Solving), 48
T-Town Treats case example, 4–5

Uber, 123
Uncertainty, in "fog of war," 24
Unified data platforms, 121
Unilever, 9
Unknown Knowns, 71, 72
Unknown Unknowns, 71, 72
Unpredictable environments, 60
Unreasonable points of view,
  hearing, 48
Unstructured data, 44
Upskilling, 31, 83
Upwork, 45

US Treasury yield, 6
Usage metrics, 114
Using connections, in LUCK
 framework, 96–97

Validation, 33
Velcro, 97
Vibe coding, 11
Vietnam War, 47
Visibility, of decision's impact, 4
Vision:
 defining, for transformation,
  107–110
 difficulties creating, 16–17
 ensuring AI technology supports,
  109
 as guide for decision making, 117
 sharing, 110
 timeline for realizing, 110
Viva Topics, 11
Volatile, uncertain, complex,
 and ambiguous (VUCA)
 environments, 98

Von Moltke, Helmuth, 25, 27

Wait-and-see approach, x, 67–68
Walmart Data Ventures, 58
Weak ties, 97
Wei-ji, 69
Windbreaker, invention of, 107
Work charts, 36
Workforce impacts, of AI
 experiments, 114
Workforce reduction, 83–84, 112
World War II, 7
W.R. Grace, 118
Wunker, Stephen, xi–xii, 35

Yucatán Peninsula, asteroid impact,
 vii–viii

Zara, 75
Zhejiang University, 59
Zipper, 107
Zoom, 9
Zuckerberg, Mark, 34

We hope you found the book both useful and enjoyable. Please leave a review on your favorite platform!

www.ingramcontent.com/pod-product-compliance
Lightning Source LLC
Chambersburg PA
CBHW041917190326
41458CB00049B/6849/J